THE RIVER OF LIFE

THE RIVER OF LIFE

MARY TANNER CANNON

XULON PRESS

Xulon Press
2301 Lucien Way #415
Maitland, FL 32751
407.339.4217
www.xulonpress.com

© 2019 by Mary Tanner Cannon

All rights reserved solely by the author. The author guarantees all contents are original and do not infringe upon the legal rights of any other person or work. No part of this book may be reproduced in any form without the permission of the author. The views expressed in this book are not necessarily those of the publisher.

Printed in the United States of America.

ISBN-13: 978-1-54567-003-3

12-8-23

Jean, Glad your coming to the tea and happy to finally meet you!

God Bless!
Love Mary

Table of Contents

Author's Dedication: ix

1. Reflecting 1
2. Church 5
3. Chores & School 7
4. Picnic & Fishing 11
5. My Dad 13
6. The Party Dress 15
7. Vacation Bible School 17
8. Mothers Birthday 21
9. High School 23
10. Graduation 27
11. Mrs. Barrett 29
12. New Job 37
13. Work Begins 45
14. Thanksgiving 49
15. My Job, On My Own 61
16. Christmas Holiday 63
17. Miss Hattie's Death 65
18. The Law Firm 69

19. Peter in The Army 75
20. Mrs. Barrett's Illness. 79
21. My Feelings for Jon 81
22. Mrs. Barrett's Cancer. 87
23. Bill's Death. 93
24. Christmas & The Proposal. 97
25. Preparations for The Wedding 101
26. My and Jon's Wedding Day 111
27. Honeymoon 119
28. The Wedding Surprise 123
29. My Dad's Heart Attack 129
30. Unexpected Surprise for Jon 135
31. Mrs. Barrett's Death. 143
32. Folks Aging 147
33. Everyone Home for Christmas 149
34. Peter & Krista 153
35. Good News 157
36. Baby Arrived. 163
37. Dad Passed Away 165
38. Deaths 167

The reason I wrote this book:. 171

Author's Dedication:

This book is dedicated to our son, James Benson Penick. Ben was born October 15, 1968 and on May 11, 2016 was diagnosed with ALS. He fought the disease for 2 ½ years and was taken home to be with the Lord on November 1, 2018.

At Ben's Memorial, he spoke through a video urging anyone who did not have a relationship with the Lord Jesus Christ to give their hearts to Him with the assurance of eternal life. Ben told the congregation a couple of days after he was diagnosed, he was in his car ready to leave for work. He prayed, "Lord, I don't feel you with me, I'm fighting this battle by myself, I need You to help me." Ben said at that moment his car filled with the Holy Spirit so much so, it was suffocating, and from that time on, the Lord gave him peace and comfort. Ben said he could not and would not let ALS go to waste, he would use it to glorify God.

Ben and his family enjoyed life after that gift from the Lord. They traveled, enjoyed each other and rarely missed a function or party. Ben went on to say, "God has a plan for our lives and it's eternal life in heaven with Him, it's a 'free' gift, all we have to do is accept it." Ben concluded, "there are great people here today who will Pray with you

THE RIVER OF LIFE

and encourage you, all you have to do is accept that opportunity."

The Memorial ended with Ben giving a wonderful Prayer, praising God for his Goodness and Mercy shown to him through his journey and thanking Him for healing his body.

Loy and I miss our son terribly, but we are assured he is with our Lord and Savior. We sincerely hope Ben's message touched someone's heart for the Lord. Ben leaves behind his lovely wife, Tiffany and two precious daughters, Jamisen and Emily and many friends and family.

Thank you and may God Bless all of you.
Mary (Tanner) Cannon

Chapter 1

Reflecting

After my beloved husband's funeral, my two daughters, their husbands, and their children went back to our house. Soon they loaded up their cars and left for their homes. Suddenly, I was alone. I had tried to imagine what this day would feel like, but never knew I would feel so empty and lost. As I stood in my living room and looked around, nothing looked familiar. How could that be? I had lived in this house over fifty years and suddenly, I felt like a stranger in my own home. My two daughters were brought home from the hospital to this house. Both girls were married in this house. We had entertained many friends, had more birthday parties, and sleepovers than I can remember. why did I feel this way? Would this fear and feeling go away with time? Would I be able to survive in this house alone? The sun was sitting low on the horizon and I knew I couldn't stay in this room and watch it go down, I felt I had to get in the car and just drive. I had no idea where I was

THE RIVER OF LIFE

going when I backed the car out of the driveway and turned up the street.

Probably thirty minutes had passed when I realized I was heading to the River Town where I grew up. I turned up the dirt road toward our old house. My car seemed to know where we were going. I passed our house; it looked so small and sad. The paint was peeling, some of the shingles were gone from the roof and the screen door hung at an angle, ready to drop. The grass and scrubs were dead, and Mother's rose garden was no longer there. I barely recognized the place. Suddenly, my heart ached for my parents, even though they had passed away years ago. I parked the car and walked down the dirt path toward the river bank. The sun was going down now, and I loved the way it flickered through the trees and sparkled on the water like flowing diamonds. Now I felt peaceful. What was it about this river that gave me such comfort? I walked closer and sat down on the large stump of a once beautiful maple tree. My memories came flooding back as I sat on that stump and thought about my childhood.

I grew up next to the River. Our family consisted of my parents, me and two little brothers.

My name is Kathryn Collier and I was twelve when the story begins, the year was 1937. I was tall for my age, a thin and gangly young girl. I had blue eyes and auburn hair, thick and slightly curly. I was in the sixth grade at our little school. It was known as Bunker Hill. The building was a two-room school house, with one teacher, Miss Hattie.

Reflecting

Peter, my oldest little brother was eight and in the third grade. He was a sweet blond with deep blue eyes and always happy. Brady, my youngest little brother was six and in the first grade. He too was a little cotton top blond, with lots of curly hair and a chubby little face. Brady was our baby and he knew how to work us all. We didn't mind, he was so sweet, you just couldn't say 'no' to him.

We were not rich, but we didn't know it. We were about the happiest people on earth. All the other families living close by were like us. We all had a small plot of ground, not enough to be considered serious farmers, just enough land to have a large truck patch and a few acres for pasture. We had two cows to provide our dairy products, a few pigs which my Dad raised for our winter meat, and a hen house full of chickens that supplied our eggs and raised young chickens to eat.

We planted green beans, sweet corn, potatoes, tomatoes, cantaloupe, watermelon and other vegetables in our truck patch. When the vegetables were ready to be harvested, my Dad and Peter filled the bed of our old truck with the fresh vegetables we had grown for sale. They headed for town early on Saturday morning when the ladies would shop. We were always excited to see them return with what we kid's thought was a wealth of money. Later, I realized it was barely enough to survive.

Chapter 2

Church

Saturday nights were filled with baths, shampoos (my hair would be rolled up in painful pin curls), all shoes polished, clothes washed, pressed, and ready for our best event of the week, "Sunday church." On the way to Church my brothers and I rode in the back of the truck. I tried hard to keep the wind from blowing my dress up and messing up my curly hair. Mother would be disappointed if we arrived at Church and my hair was in an upheaval mess. I never wanted to disappoint my Mother. She was a small, kind faced woman with a rather plain look, but she had the most amazing, sparkling blue eyes. Her voice was soft and kind. I will never forget her hands. They were small but a bit crooked from all the hard work she did to keep our family going. I would watch her on wash day as she rubbed the clothes back and forth on her wash board and then wrung the water out with those tiny, crooked hands. My Mother never complained; she always seemed happy and content. However, as I look back now, I realize what a hardship life was

THE RIVER OF LIFE

for both my Mother and Dad. When we would sit down to eat our meals, my Dad would say the most amazing Prayer. My parents were both so thankful to God for what He had given them, and they were always ready to praise Him.

Church for my family and the families who lived along the river was our time of praising the Lord. We enjoyed fellowshipping, visiting and always lots of food on Sunday after services.

Our Church building was small, but beautiful. There was an older gentleman in our congregation who was a woodworking marvel. He owned a small woodworking shop where he made beautiful furniture, Mr. Wilson was his name.

Mr. Wilson made the Church pews, the podium, the Communion table and tall candle sticks that flanked each side of the table. He even carved the beautiful passage from scripture on the front of the Communion table, which read 'DO THIS IN REMEMBRANCE OF ME'.

Chapter 3

Chores & School

My brothers and I walked to school unless it was bad weather. Then, when it was rainy or cold, my Dad would take us in the truck. There was no school bus that we could ride.

Our teacher, Miss Hattie was a tall, kind, and very gentle woman, but she was also stern. She taught the little kids first.

We older kids swept the floor in the big room and made sure all the little kids had hung up their coats and hats. We also put their boots on the shelf provided for them. We lined the desks in a straight row and dusted the erasers outside. That activity would always turn into a bit of a fun game. Next, we took an old lard bucket, filled with water, and washed the blackboard. The older boys would carry in loads of wood for the stove and continued to stoke it to keep both rooms warm. When Miss Hattie was finished teaching the little kids, the big room would be ready for our class to begin. She wanted to make sure our little minds absorbed every word and problem she put before us, and

THE RIVER OF LIFE

she didn't stop until we had learned each lesson. The hardest was math multiplication tables but she drilled us until we had mastered them.

Chores were a must for the kids who lived along the river bank. My job was to carry in the wood for Mothers' cook stove and coal for the heating stove in our small living room. I also gathered the eggs. Sometimes one of the hens would still be on her warm nest. When I encouraged her to get up, she protested by trying to peck me. Often, I dropped my egg basket and ran to the house. I was scared to death of those chickens. At those times, Mother followed me back to the hen house and very gently slide her small hand under the chicken to get the eggs. The chicken seemed to expect her. After Mother gathered the eggs, the hen would turn her head to one side and look at me with one of those little scary eyes. I never mastered the art of egg gathering.

Peter and Brady had to go down into the pasture and bring the cows up for the nightly milking. Peter would get a tree limb from the fence row and swing it violently at the cows. When the cows were heading toward the barn, he slowed his running to a fast walk. Brady was bringing up the rear, swinging his stick back and forth, hitting the tall grass and weeds with a vengeance.

Each March when the winter snow had finally melted, and spring was approaching, my brothers and I were excited to play along the river bank. We got our cane fishing poles with line and hook, and away we went to fish in the river. My mother always fixed us a little picnic lunch of jelly and

Chores & School

biscuit sandwiches in a small lard bucket. For a special treat, she surprised us by including chocolate rolls. These were made from a bit of leftover biscuit dough, sprinkled with sugar and coco powder rolled up and baked to a golden brown. Yum, yum! those were the best things we ever ate.

Chapter 4

Picnic & Fishing

One bright and warm sunny afternoon, we had our picnic under a beautiful maple tree. After eating, we walked back to the river bank for a little fishing fun. Mother always cautioned us not to get too close to the banks edge as the earth underneath would be wet and soft and give way. We three were excited for our first fishing fun of the summer. Our hooks were in the water for a few minutes when I noticed my little brother was starting to slide toward the water. Just as his little bare feet were going in and he was wet just below his overall pockets, I grabbed him by his suspenders and pulled him back onto the bank. He began to whimper and cry, Mama will be mad at me for getting my clothes wet and muddy. His little chubby face became stained with streams of tears. I couldn't bear his pain. "Don't worry," I told him, "I will take care of it."

Well, it looked like fishing was over. We gathered up our poles, lunch bucket, and shoes and headed for home. Mother was in the kitchen, so I

THE RIVER OF LIFE

took my little brother around to the back porch and removed his little muddy overalls. I motioned for him to be quite as we both tiptoed to our bedroom. I quietly opened his drawer and got him some dry underpants and overalls. I quickly dressed him, and we quietly tiptoed out the back door.

I gathered up his wet and muddy clothes and headed for the wash house. I pumped a bucket of water and dowsed the underpants and overall back and forth in the bucket until the muddy residue was gone, emptied the mud water from the bucket and quickly put everything back in place. I hung the clothes in the back of the wash house hoping they would dry overnight; I would retrieve them in the morning. My precious little brother looked up at me with a broad smile and eyes watering, reached up his little arms and said, "I love you Sissy". I love you too sweetheart, as we headed back to the house for supper.

Chapter 5

My Dad

Our Dad was a strong built, tanned faced, good looking man. He had a rugged but gentle look about him with piercing blue eyes. He adored our Mother. You could see the way he looked at her and, would touch the back of her hair as he walked past her chair.

In the evenings, we sat by the stove in the living room and Dad would read from the Bible to us with light from a kerosene lamp while Mother would sew or mend. Our Christian upbringing was most important to my parents, above schooling or making money. I think that is why we were always so happy and content; we lived by God's word. If my parents ever worried about money or the lack of it, we *kids* never knew it. There was never talk of being poor or not having enough. We had each other and all the love anyone could want.

Chapter 6

The Party Dress

Life by the river was simple and uncomplicated. I remember when I was thirteen years old, being invited to my first birthday party by one of the girls who went to our Church. Her family had a much larger house than we and they even had a car. Her mother was always dressed in an outfit that came from the dress shop in town. We, my Mom and I, wore dresses my Mother made from fabric she purchased from the grocery store, or flour sack material. When I was invited to the party, Mother said she would make me a new dress. I was very excited, but there was one problem. The material which held the flour in our pantry was not very pretty. I would look every few days to see if the flour was almost gone from that ugly pattern sack. Finally, the day arrived. It was time to get the fabric for my party dress.

Mother and I went into town with my Dad and brothers to get our food supply at the local grocery store. I ran as fast as I could to the back of the store where the sacks of flour were stacked neatly in one corner. I ran my eyes up and down, back and forth, searching for just the right material for my party dress. Finally, I spotted it, a soft pink plaid with tiny pink rosebuds sporadically placed on the plaid pattern. I loved it! I ran back to the front of the store where my Mother was shopping and shouted, "I found it Mother, you're going to love it too." We slowly followed the store clerk to the back corner of the store and I excitedly pointed to the sack I had fallen in love with. The clerk said, "Wow, does it have to be that one?" It was practically on the very bottom of a large stack. I looked disappointed at his reluctance to pulling it out, then he began to smile and said, "no problem, we can get that sack for you." I was elated. We arrived back home and quickly Mother opened the sack of flour, dumping it from the beautiful sack into the ugly sack. She washed the fabric and started my new dress. I always stood on the other side of the old treadle sewing machine every time my Mother sat down to sew, and I watched every stitch until my dress was finished. Mother had saved some pink ribbon and white lace from a dress she had found at a garage sale. She carefully removed it from the worn dress. It was perfectly placed on my dress and wow, how beautiful was that. Mother had one small piece of pink ribbon which she made a bow for the back of my pulled up, long dark hair. I felt like a princess. These many, many years later, I can still picture that pretty party dress.

Chapter 7

Vacation Bible School

The years seemed to fly by, and we three kids grew up quickly. I would be going into town to the High School, leaving my little brothers back at our little schoolhouse. I was sad because I had always been there to watch after them and handle any bumps or hurt feelings. I convinced myself they would be fine.

Our school had a small graduation for the six of us older kids who would be moving on to High School. It was exciting but also a bit sad. We would not be able to see Miss Hattie every day and would not be as carefully tutored in the new school. Miss Hattie seemed sad to see us leave too.

I will never forget the beautiful dress Miss Hattie wore to our graduation. It was navy blue with long sleeves and lovely lace carefully placed around the white collar and cuffs. She looked amazing. Miss Hattie was older now in her 70's, but you would never know it the way she played with us at recess. She also invented fun games when the weather was cold or rainy and we had

THE RIVER OF LIFE

to play inside. I thought that if I ever knew success, I would owe it all to Miss Hattie's teaching and my parent's Christian training. They made sure we three kids had high morals and knew right from wrong.

School was out for the summer and we had lots of fun activities planned which included picnics, fishing and tending the roses my Mother so lovingly planted in our yard. When summer days were hot, I pumped buckets of water for Mothers flowers. They were so beautiful, and Mother loved her rose garden.

Growing up we had a lot of Church functions. Vacation Bible School was one of our favorite summer events. The Church women prepared crafts, games and great snacks. We gathered in front of our little Church each morning, lined up in straight rows and sang some songs. After singing, our Pastor prayed for us to learn about Jesus and that we would all grow up to love and serve Him. Then, we all marched very orderly into the Church building. We went to different corners of the little Church, according to our ages, where one of the women would teach us about the Lord. We read scriptures, and each child took a scripture verse home to memorize overnight, and to recite it the next day in our VBS class. We made wonderful crafts too.

I remember one year, Ms. Roberta took eight, twelve-year-old students to her house. In her back yard, she had a grape vineyard. She told us to select one large grape leaf and two smaller ones from the vines. She then had us place all the

Vacation Bible School

leaves onto a flatten ball of clay. She instructed us to very gently take our little knife-like tools and cut the outside clay away from the leaves and to turn up the outside edges of the larger leaf of clay making a little dish. The next step was to make little balls of clay to represent grapes and attach the two smaller clay leaves to the bunch of grapes on the top edge of our little dish. We also made a round piece of clay about the size of half a pencil, crooked it, and placed it beside the grape bunches for a handle. How lovely this would be! I couldn't wait to finish mine for my Mother. She would be so thrilled. We then painted our little dishes. Perfect! I loved it. Our little treasures were then put in a kiln and fired. We didn't see them for a few days, but when they came back, I couldn't believe my eyes. If I hadn't scratched my name on the back of my little dish, I would have never recognized it. It was a beautiful shade of dark greenish/brown with the purple grapes and green leaves.

    Knowing about porcelain paints, the colors you use to paint, are not the colors you end up with. It was amazing. My heart pounded as I was now visualizing my Mothers excitement when I presented my gift to her for her upcoming birthday. We made other crafts in VBS, but none could ever be as beautiful as that little dish. I continued to love Ms. Roberta, until well into her 90's, she went to be with Jesus.

Chapter 8

Mothers Birthday

VBS was over and summer started to wind down. My Mothers' birthday was in late July and her awaited birthday had finally arrived. I had carefully hidden away my little dish and was anxiously waiting to give her the treasure I had made for her.

Wrapping paper was not available so I went to Mothers sewing machine drawer and found a beautiful piece of lilac material which had violets and green leaves all over it. That would be perfect for wrapping my dish to give Mother. I carefully wrapped the fabric around the little dish and tied it with a piece of string; I was ready for Mothers' birthday. We didn't have a birthday cake, but there were some oatmeal cookies in the cookie jar. I took out five cookies and placed them on one of Mothers' best plates. I sit the cookies beside my gift on the kitchen table.

Mother had finished cleaning the kitchen after our evening meal and she and Dad were sitting on the porch enjoying the cool breeze after a very

THE RIVER OF LIFE

warm summer day. I went out on the porch and very nervously invited them inside.

When Mother and Dad entered the kitchen, my brothers and I were positioned on the other side of the table and began to sing 'Happy Birthday' to Mother. She looked very surprised and Dad was wearing a broad proud smile knowing we had tried to make this very special for our loving Mother.

She looked at the little fabric wrapped present on the table. "Honey, what is in the package?" as she looked at me. "It's for you Mother, unwrap it and see," I said anxiously. She carefully picked the package up and began to meticulously untie the string and slowly removed the lilac fabric. "Oh, my goodness," she shrieked, how beautiful! I have never seen anything as lovely in my life. I made it at VBS this year Mother, and I knew before I had finished it; it would be perfect for your birthday. I do hope you like it. "More than like it, I love it!" Mother said. She grabbed me and gave a tight squeezing hug, then onto my brothers with the same hugs and kisses for all of us.

She took the little dish over to the only table we had in the living room and placed it carefully by the kerosene lamp. "Perfect," she said as we all prepared for a wonderful night's sleep after a beautiful Birthday.

Chapter 9

High School

Fall was quickly approaching, days grew shorter, and the nights began to get cooler. The trees down by the river had all taken on beautiful hues of golden yellow, orange, and bright red. Words cannot express the beauty of the colorful river bank, and the beautiful maple tree which stood close to the river was also a sight to behold. The grass was still green as we had not had a hard frost yet so the green with the other colors was beautiful. That's when you know that God is responsible for the beauty of our earth; it just makes you feel thankful and so much closer to Him.

Fall also brought me closer to beginning High School in town. I was excited but also a bit apprehensive. The only kids I would know were the other five I had graduated with a few months earlier, but I also looked forward to making new friends. Mother had made me some new skirts, blouses, and the last time she went into town had also bought me some new socks. So, I was all set for school to begin.

THE RIVER OF LIFE

The first day of school arrived and I was still home when my brothers were preparing for their walk down the road to their two-room schoolhouse. "You take care of Brady," I told Peter. If it storms, make sure Miss Hattie remembers he gets really scared and you might have to go to the little room and be with him. Also, tell Miss Hattie I will miss her but will still see her at Church, and will have lots to tell her. "Don't worry Sis, Brady will be fine, and I'll be sure to tell Miss Hattie how much you will miss her," Peter yelled over his shoulder as he slammed the screen door.

The High School had a bus, but I still had to walk about half a mile to the bus stop. I started early; I sure didn't want to miss that bus the first day. Mother had made a wonderful lunch for me and I was wearing one of my new skirts and a blouse. Mother had fixed my hair and pulled it up high in the back and let me wear her pretty barrette. I felt on top of the world.

When we arrived at school there was a group of girls standing by a tree in front of the school. I started to walk toward them and one of the girls came to meet me. She introduced herself. "Hi, I'm Sarah." "Hello, my name is Kathryn, I replied." She told me it was her first day at this school too. She and her family had moved to our little town from out of state. I was relieved to know I would not be the only one looking for my class. The day went by quickly and it was time to get back on the bus. I waved goodbye to my new friend Sarah, and assured her I would see her tomorrow.

High School

I was excited to get home and tell Mother and Dad about my new friend, about my day, and to find out how my little brothers made it on their first day without me. To my surprise, they did just fine. I was happy as I had thought of them several times during the day and was a bit worried that all would not be well. I had noticed the wind was getting up and there were a couple of dark clouds. But, by the time school was over, the wind had calmed, and the clouds had disappeared. I knew then Brady would be fine.

Chapter 10

Graduation

Four years of high school passed quickly, and it would soon be time for me to graduate. Sarah and I had remained best friends all through High School and made vows to always keep in touch. Sarah had said she was going to the city which was about 160 miles from our little town. She had an aunt and some cousins she could stay with while she looked for work. We said our goodbye, hugged and cried while knowing in our hearts our friendship would always continue and we would see each other at some time in the future.

Peter started High School the fall after my graduation. That meant Brady would be by himself at the two-room Country School, but he was twelve now so I knew he would be fine. He seemed to grow up so fast those past four years.

I had planned to move about 60 miles to the nearest city after graduation and look for work. Mother was a bit apprehensive, but Dad assured her I would be fine. I wasn't so sure. This would be the first time I had been away from home and,

THE RIVER OF LIFE

I was really a home body. I was very close to my family and would miss them terribly, but I knew it was time for me to make my transition to adulthood

    We graduated on a Friday night, there were 47 of us. Everyone was excited and chatting about their futures. A lot of the kids were going to stay around our little town and either look for work or help their parents with their truck patches. Although I loved living by the river bank, I wanted to see what the world had to offer a shy country girl from the River.

Chapter 11

Mrs. Barrett

I stayed home for the remainder of the summer helping my parents with the fruits and vegetables, but September was quickly approaching. I wanted to try to land a job before winter. Mother had a high school friend who lived in the city, her name was Mrs. Barrett. Mother had written to her asking if I could possibly stay with her for a few weeks until I found a job and a place to live. Mrs. Barrett graciously consented to my visit, which would be short, I had hoped. I didn't want to impose on her.

As the bus approached my stop, I stepped off and began to walk down the street looking for Mrs. Barrett's address. Suddenly, I saw it. What a lovely home. I couldn't believe I was going to be fortunate enough to stay in such a beautiful atmosphere. It was a white single-story bungalow with green shutters, and a large front porch surrounded by lush flower beds. The house was encircled by a white picket fence holding up an array of various colors of climbing rose bushes. I stepped onto the

THE RIVER OF LIFE

front porch and softly knocked at the door. Mrs. Barrett answered. "Hello, I'm Kathryn Collier, I said in a shy voice." "Hello Kathryn, I've been expecting you," Mrs. Barrett said as she welcomed me in. "This is so nice of you to allow me to stay with you, Mrs. Barrett." I'm happy to have you Kathryn, I was thrilled to hear from Ethel asking if you could stay with me. After a few minutes of getting acquainted, Mrs. Barrett showed me to a comfortable bedroom. She lived alone so she seemed happy to have someone around to talk with and cook for. That would work for me. I arrived in the city on a Friday afternoon and quickly settled into my room. We had a light dinner and then sat on her lovely porch enjoying the fall breeze.

Saturday, I woke early and asked where I could buy a newspaper. Mrs. Barrett directed me to the newspaper office, and I rushed down to get a paper so I could start my job hunt. When I returned home, she had a lovely breakfast ready and served it on the back porch that overlooked a beautiful lush garden. There were a lot of colorful fall mums and other flowers still hanging on before the first frost would come and take them.

After breakfast had been cleared away, I spread out my newspaper and began to scan the 'Want Ads'. It looked like there were a lot of jobs available and surely one would be just right for me. I had taken shorthand and typing both my junior and senior years in high school and had become skilled at both, so I was interested in finding a steno-typist position. I circled four so, come Monday morning, I would start my quest.

Mrs. Barrett

Monday morning came. I was up early and excited to start my job hunt. Mrs. Barrett had also gotten up early and prepared a light breakfast for us. We both had a poached egg, toast and tea. I was very grateful as I knew my day would involve a lot of walking. I would have to take the bus to two of the job interviews. However, two of them were within walking distant of Mrs. Barrett's house. It would be great to be able to walk to work. I could get some exercise each day, plus save the money it would cost to buy bus tokens.

I had saved some of the money our Church friends had given me as a graduation gift. Mother and I had gone into town to the dress shop and purchased a nice herringbone suit. It was in shades of light brown. I also had a cream cotton blouse which I wore under it. I grabbed my white gloves and hat, feeling I was ready to face the corporate world.

My first stop was at the Newspaper Office. I had noticed when I purchased the newspaper on Saturday, a sign in the window stating, 'Help Wanted'. It was for a receptionist/typist. I knew typing was one of my strong suits but receptionist, I wasn't so sure. I had not used a phone much and had no experience in meeting the public, but hey, I was ready to learn and tackle any job I was given.

I entered the office approaching the front desk. There was an older woman with mousey grey hair put up in a tight bun, sitting at the desk. Without lifting her head she said, "Yes, can I help you?" I was taken back a bit by what seemed to be a rude jester. I'm here to put in for your job opening

THE RIVER OF LIFE

madam. "Don't call me madam," she said without again lifting her head. She handed me a piece of paper and pencil. Fill this out and return it to me. "Thank you," I said in a soft defeated voice.

As I took my chair and began to fill out the application, my thoughts went back to my encounter with the lady at the front desk. If I had that job, I thought to myself, I would be a bit more personal and not seem like I got up on the wrong side of the bed. I hoped if I did get this job, she would not be my boss. However, I had always been able to get along with everyone and she would be no exception. It just might take some extra work on my part, but I was up for the challenge. I finished with the application and went back to the front desk. I stood there for what seemed to be at least 60 seconds before she finally acknowledged me. She reached out her hand for my application and quickly scanned both sides and said in a gruff voice, "check back in a week and we will let you know." Again, she didn't bother to raise her head. I'll bet she couldn't pick me out of a line up if her life depended on it. Anyway, I had other job possibilities I was going to check out.

The second job on my list was in a small Law Firm, it too was within walking distance of Mrs. Barrett's house. When I arrived at the office address, it was very neat on the outside. It had two large plate glass windows on each side of a wooden door. On each window in large letters were the words ATTORNEYS AT LAW – JONATHAN DAVIS & CURTIS SIMMONS. There were two potted green plants on each side of the beautiful

Mrs. Barrett

wood door. The inside was very neat and professional. There were two brown leather couches, three leather chairs and a couple of tables with nice lamps in the room. There was a coffee table between the couches where several magazines were neatly placed. In the corner of the room was a tall potted tree. The receptionist desk was a dark mahogany wood with a leather chair which matched the chairs and couches in the reception area. Behind the desk was a beautiful woman with long dark hair and a striking sweet smile. She greeted me with a warm friendly "hello," may I help you? "Yes," I said, "I'm here to apply for the steno/typist position listed in the paper." "Oh great," she said, as she stood and turned toward a tall dark grey filing cabinet, opened a drawer and pulled out a piece of paper, walked back to her desk, picked up a pencil and handed it to me. Please complete this application and, when you are finished, I will let Mr. Davis know. He will be the attorney interviewing you. As I sat down and started to complete the application, I had noticed the young woman was expecting a baby. I wondered if it's her position they are filling. I assumed she would not be returning to work after her maternity leave.

    I took my time and completed the application, going back over every question to make sure I had not made any errors, and then returned to the desk to give the paper and pencil to the nice young lady. She took it from my hand and gave me a sweet assuring smile. Don't be nervous, Mr. Davis is a very gentle person and easy to work for. They both are. Her reassurance had put me at ease, so I casually picked up one of the magazines and not really looking at it, began to flip the pages. I was just thinking how great it would be to work in this nice office surrounded by such pretty things and the calm feeling the room seemed to generate.

I hadn't waited long when a tall man with dark wavy hair and deep brown eyes, wearing a navy suit, white shirt and red striped tie, came out of one of the offices and greeted me. The young woman at the desk said as she smiled, "Mr. Davis will see you now." I stood and thanked her. Mr. Davis reached out his hand for mine and said, "What's your name?" "Kathryn Collier," I replied as he shook my hand. "Come into my office and have a seat." "Thank you." I knew he could tell I was nervous, so the conversation started with; So Kathryn, have you lived in the City long? I have only been here a few days. I'm staying with one of my Mothers friends until I can get my own place. I do love the city though; everyone seems to be going someplace. "That's for sure," he said with a soft chuckle, you should see it at rush hour.

Well Miss Collier, I see by your application that you have graduated High School with honors and high scores in shorthand and typing. We are looking for someone of your caliber who is accomplished in these two areas. There will also be some filing, answering the phone, making appointments for our clients as well as sitting in on my and Curtis's morning sessions when we go over our cases. At that time, we would like for you to takes notes, type them up and put them in our client's files. Does that sound like something you would be interested in doing, he asked? "Yes of course," I said quickly. This is just the job I was hoping for. I love typing and taking shorthand and although I don't have filing or phone experience, I'm sure I could learn if given the opportunity. Well, tell you what Miss Collier, I will talk with my partner Curtis, and if you could come back tomorrow afternoon say around 2:00 p.m., we will have an answer for you. "I will be glad to," I replied, tomorrow at 2:00 p.m., I will be here and thank you very much. "You're quite welcome," see you tomorrow, as he turned and went back into the office behind another beautiful frosted glass door, which said, JONATHAN DAVIS, ATTORNEY AT LAW.

I turned and started to leave when the young lady said, "good luck, I hope you get the job." "Thanks, I hope I do too. See you tomorrow at 2:00 p.m.," as I reached for the large chrome handle on the pretty wood door.

As I made my way down the street back to Mrs. Barrett's house, I prayed to God that if this is where He wants me, I would really like to have this job. It's all up to you Father, put me and use me where You would have me.

Chapter 12

New Job

I decided not to check into the other two jobs I had circled on the newspaper until after 2:00 p.m. tomorrow. If this was not the job I was meant to have, I would buy some bus tokens and go to the other two places. But for now, I felt good.

I arrived back at Mrs. Barrett's house and she greeted me from the front porch. "Sit down dear and have a glass of lemonade," she said. I saw you coming down the street and had just made a cool pitcher. "Well", she said, looking puzzled. "Any luck today?"

I had gone to two places, I told her. The first was the Newspaper Office and the second was the Law Office of Davis and Simmons. I put in applications at both places and the lady at the Newspaper Office said check back in a week, however, the Law office said to come back tomorrow at 2:00 p.m. I feel good about the Law Office position, they were very nice, and it would be wonderful to be able to walk to work. Across the street from the office is a nice little park with several big shady

THE RIVER OF LIFE

oak trees with park benches and tables where I could go have my lunch. "Yes", I know that park, Mrs. Barrett said, it is very nice. I used to take my dog down there and walk him in the cool grass before he passed away last year. Well Kathryn, I hope you get the job. Remember, you are more than welcome to stay with me until you can get your own place. I love having you; I sometime get lonesome since I lost my little dog. I have threatened to get another one, but I get so attached, I'm not sure I could take going through that again. Mrs. Barrett and I sat on the porch and enjoyed the cool breeze and fresh lemonade for quite some time.

I excused myself and went into my room to write my family a letter. I knew they would be anxious to hear from me. My family didn't have a phone, however, if there was an emergency, the local grocery store in our little town delivers the message to the families living along the river. The folks would get my letter in about 4 days, so that would be fine. I didn't have that much to tell them, I wasn't assured of the job at the Law Office yet, but I just wanted to let them know I was fine, and Mrs. Barrett and I were getting along great. She has been so gracious and kind to me.

However, I was already missing them. I knew by this time Mother was starting the evening meal, Dad was finishing up the nightly milking, and my little brothers were getting their homework. I could close my eyes and picture the calm and serenity of our little home. I probably wouldn't go home until Thanksgiving. That would be two months. I had not been away from my parents for even a week, let

New Job

alone two months. My goal was to focus on my job and helping Mrs. Barrett around the house.

When I first arrived, I had asked Mrs. Barrett if she went to Church. "Oh yes," she said, "I go to the big Baptist Church down on the corner of Main and Alice Streets. I would be very happy for you to go with me."

On the following Sunday morning, we had some toast and tea and got ready for Church. I put on one of my nice skirts and blouses and we walked down the street to the large brown Church building. It was much larger and fancier than our little country Church, but no more beautiful than our handmade pews and all. I did love the new Church though; the choir members wore lovely deep red robes and sang some beautiful old hymns I was familiar with. The Pastor was a good speaker, as well. I am looking forward to going again with Mrs. Barrett. I noticed a lot of young people, so there is probably a class for my age group. I want to get involved in Church; I would miss not being among people who are serving the Lord.

Tuesday morning came, and I was excited for my 2:00 p.m. appointment. I put on my suit skirt with just my cream blouse without my jacket. It was mid-September, but the days were still warm. I just hoped I looked professional enough for my appointment.

I arrived at Mr. Davis office at 1:50 p.m. When I walked in the young woman at the desk greeted me again with a pleasant smile. "Good afternoon," she said, "how are you today?" "Good, it's so nice out today, I just love the cool fall weather," I said

THE RIVER OF LIFE

with a smile. "Please make yourself comfortable, Mr. Davis is on a conference call, but he will be with you shortly," she said. "Thank you, I don't mind waiting."

The young woman started the conversation I had wondered about. "I will be leaving my job after Thanksgiving to have my baby and have decided to stay home. My husband works as a logger and we think we can survive on one income while our baby is small," she stated. "That will be nice," I told her. I'm sure, this is an exciting time for you and your husband. "Yes, very much so," she said. We have been waiting for this baby for six years, so yes, we are anxious. "I will pray for a healthy baby and quick delivery," I told her. "I really appreciate that," she said with a warm smile.

In a few minutes, the door to Mr. Davis office opened and he stepped out. "Well, looks like we didn't scare you off yesterday, glad to see you came back." "Thank you for seeing me," I said shyly as we both entered his office and he shut the door behind us. Please have a seat, Miss Collier, and we will go over a few things. My partner and I have discussed your qualifications and we both feel you would be a good candidate for filling our position. Our present secretary Emily, will be with us until Thanksgiving to show you the ropes. We have agreed on a starting salary for you if you choose to accept it and you will be reviewed in six months for a salary increase. He wrote down a figure on a piece of paper and slowly pushed it across his desk toward me. This is the amount Curtis and I have agreed to start if this is agreeable.

New Job

I looked at the paper and couldn't believe my eyes. They were willing to pay me more a month than my family would make in three months from selling fruits and vegetables out of the truck patch. My first thought was that I would make enough to send my folks some money from time to time. I was so excited my heart was racing. "Well, Miss Collier, is that a yes? Are you willing to take on this job for a couple of poor practicing attorneys?" "Oh yes," Mr. Davis, "I am very happy to accept this position. Thank you so much." "Ok then," Mr. Davis said as he slowly stood up from his leather chair. "Guess we'll see you in the morning at 9:00 a.m. Oh by the way, I failed to tell you your hours. We work from 9:00 a.m. until 5:00 p.m., five days a week. We are closed on Saturday and Sunday. Sometimes Curtis and I come into the office on Saturday for a couple of hours if we have a big case. We have been known to work seven days a week and into the nights, but that is not too often. You won't have to be here. As I got up to leave, Mr. Davis extended his hand to me and with a firm hand shake said, "welcome aboard Miss Collier, I hope you enjoy this job and you won't allow Curtis and me to make you crazy." We both laughed as I turned to leave his office. "Thanks again Mr. Davis," I said as I quickly turned back to him then left his office and closed his door. The young woman at the front desk was wearing a big smile. "Well Miss Collier, looks like you have yourself a job. By the way, my name is Emily James." "Hi Emily, call me Kathryn." "I'm sure we will get along fine Kathryn," she said with a grin. "I look forward to helping you learn the

THE RIVER OF LIFE

business, it's fun, you'll see. I have truly enjoyed my five years I have worked for Mr. Davis and Mr. Simmons, you will too, they are very kind and easy going." "Good," I said I'm excited. "I'll see you in the morning Emily." "Great" she said, as I closed the office door and headed to Mrs. Barrett's house.

When I arrived back at Mrs. Barrett's she was in the living room reading her Bible. She looked up, removing her glasses, and said, "well, what's the good news?" "I got the job," I shrieked. "Halleluiah, Praise God," she shouted. "That's wonderful Kathryn. I am very proud of you and I know your Mother and Dad will be as well."

"Mrs. Barrett, I've been thinking about our arrangement of you allowing me to stay with you. I truly enjoy being able to stay in your lovely home, however, I was wondering if you would permit me to rent my room. Of course, if you would rather not, I could certainly look for a place elsewhere. I was just thinking; it could be a little financial help for you and I sure do love being with you, and so enjoy your company. Tell you what; you bounce that idea around in your head for a couple of days, then you can let me know." "I certainly don't want to be a burden to you." "Kathryn Collier, I don't have to bounce it around for a couple of days, I can tell you right this minute, I would love nothing better than to have you be permanent in that room. But please, let's don't worry about rent money until you have worked at least a month, deal?" "Ok," I said reluctantly, "it's a deal!" "I'm going in and write my family a letter telling them the good news Mrs. Barrett."

New Job

"Ok, dinner will be ready in about an hour. Hope you are hungry; I have cooked us a good meal."

I went into my room, opened the drawer of the little desk Mrs. Barrett had provided for my room and took out a piece of note paper and pencil. I excitedly penned my good news about the job at the Law Firm on the note paper. I told my parents about Mrs. Barrett's and my arrangement and how much I missed them. I put the piece of paper in an envelope and sealed it with a kiss. I had brought some stamps with me, so I quickly walked a couple of blocks to a mailbox and dropped the letter inside. I hurried back to Mrs. Barrett's as I knew she would be putting dinner on the table. This has been a wonderful day I thought to myself and I praise God for His Goodness and for giving me a job.

Mrs. Barrett had a wonderful dinner prepared and we both enjoyed conversation about my exciting day. She had asked me to say the blessing before dinner which gave me an opportunity to thank God for such a wonderful experience and I asked Him to continue to be with me and help me do the best job at the Law Firm I could possibly do. I also thanked Him for Mrs. Barrett and my arrangement and asked Him to bless Mrs. Barrett and her home as well. "A big amen to that Kathryn! We all need God's constant blessings."

We finished our meal, continued to chat as we both cleaned the kitchen. Mrs. Barrett retired to the living room where she would always sit in her overstuffed floral-patterned chair and had her evening devotion. I had said goodnight to Mrs. Barrett

THE RIVER OF LIFE

and went to my room. I wanted to pick out my clothes for tomorrow and get a good night's sleep. I wanted to be the best I could be for my first day as a Steno/Typist.

Chapter 13

Work Begins

I woke early, took my bath and got dressed. Mrs. Barrett had prepared our breakfast of poached egg, tea & toast. She had also fixed a light lunch for me to take to work. "Mrs. Barrett, please, you don't need to prepare a lunch for me, I can do it." "Well, I wanted to do it for you this morning Kathryn, I hope it will be something you will enjoy." "Oh, I'm sure I will enjoy it." "Thank you so much." I was dressed in an attractive outfit of a skirt and blouse. After breakfast, I went back to my room and grabbed my sweater and hand bag. The mornings are starting to get cool now, close to the end of September. Excited, I left Mrs. Barrett's house and began my walk to work. This was a good time to have my morning talk with God.

I arrived at the Law Firm and Emily was just putting her jacket and hand bag away. "Good Morning Kathryn how are you doing?" Emily greeted with a sweet smile. "I'm doing great, ready to start learning." You can put your things in this closet; there are hangers in there for your sweater and a

THE RIVER OF LIFE

shelf where you can put your hand bag and lunch, Emily said as she began to get supplies from the drawer in her desk. Mr. Davis brought this chair from his office for you. I also have a pad and some pencils, she said as we both sit down in our chairs. Great, I want to take some good notes.

Emily and I started our training session and before I knew it, it was lunch time. "Well Kathryn, how about stopping for lunch?" "Wonderful! Mrs. Barrett, the lady I'm staying with, has prepared my lunch. I am getting rather hungry, and anxious to see what she sent, she is a fabulous cook." "Well," Emily stated, "I usually walk across the street to the little park and relax under one of those big oak trees." "That's exactly where I thought I would take my lunch yesterday after Mr. Davis hired me." "Let's go," Emily said, and to the park we went. It was shady, cool and relaxing. Emily told me about herself and her husband, how they had wanted to have a baby for so long and finally after many years, they were being blessed with a little one. We soon walked back to the office and finished my first day.

The next seven weeks flew by and it was time for Emily's last day at the Law Firm. She and I had become great friends. One afternoon after work, I had walked down to a children's shop. I purchased two pairs of little sleepers, some bibs, socks and a card for Emily. The store clerk wrapped them in a box with sweet paper, little angels sleeping on soft white clouds. I wrote some words of encouragement on the card, sealed it and slid it under the yellow ribbon on the package. On Emily's last day,

Work Begins

I arrived at the office first and placed my package on her desk. Mr. Davis and Mr. Simmons had put a beautiful bouquet of flowers on her desk as well. It was a lovely basket of probably ten different varieties *of* flowers, all in white; it was a going away gift for Emily. We had all gathered around Emily's desk when she arrived and as usual, she came in with a sweet smile and seemingly embarrassed at all the hoop-la. "Well," Mr. Davis started talking first, "looks like we won't have to put up with you much longer," laughing softly. She smiled shyly. "I will miss all of you so much, but I promise to drop in from time to time to say hello and show off my little bundle of joy." "You better," Mr. Simmons said as he begin to laugh loudly, or we'll be sending the 'law' after you. We all laughed, and Emily thanked us again. The men went into their offices and Emily sat down at her desk to open my package. "Oh, I love what you gave me Kathryn, this was so thoughtful of you and these are all things I can certainly use. I do want you to visit me and the baby when I get home from the hospital and you can meet my husband Tim. He has heard so much about you, he feels like he knows you already." "I can't wait to meet him and your new little one Emily. But right now, I just want to thank you for your patience in training me. I hope I won't disappoint Mr. Davis and Mr. Simmons, and I can be as efficient as you have been." "You will be Kathryn, I'm positive of it," as Emily gave me a sweet hug.

Chapter 14

Thanksgiving

Thanksgiving was quickly approaching, and I was getting excited to go home and see my family. I had been begging Mrs. Barrett to go home with me for the holiday. I didn't want her to be alone. She had gotten used to me being here and it would just be too lonesome for her. She kept saying, "I don't want to impose on your family, I know your family will want to spend the time with just you." "Nonsense," I told her, my Mother would be thrilled to see you, and after all, you have never met my Dad and little brothers. Please, I begged her. "Oh ok," she said, "but I just don't want to be a bother." You won't Mrs. Barrett, never.

Mrs. Barrett and I boarded the bus for the hour trip to our little town. I had sent the folks a note letting them know what time the bus was arriving so Dad could pick us up. I had not told them Mrs. Barrett was coming with me. Mother will be totally surprised and grateful to have Mrs. Barrett. I can't wait to see the look on her face. The bus pulled into the station and I could already see my Dad

THE RIVER OF LIFE

standing by our old truck. He began to wave, although, I knew he couldn't see me. Quickly, Mrs. Barrett and I lined up to get off, grabbing our small bags and headed for the door. Dad was walking toward us when we got off. I couldn't help but run and jump into his arms. "Kathryn, sweetheart," he said, "we have really missed our little girl." "I have missed you too Dad, more than you can imagine. Dad, this is Mrs. Barrett who has so graciously allowed me to take over her house." "Oh stop it," Mrs. Barrett said as she extended her hand to shake Dad's. "Well well, Carol Ann Barrett, I have heard about you ever since I married Ethel and finally getting to meet you is a real honor. Ethel will be thrilled out of her socks when she sees you, I am so glad you came for Thanksgiving. This is going to be a glorious holiday for all of us," Dad continued. "Well, I have certainly heard all about you these past few weeks and it's good to finally meet you too," Mrs. Barrett said.

We loaded our things into Dad's truck, got in and started toward home. "This is beautiful country," Mrs. Barrett said; "now I know why you were so homesick Kathryn." "Yes, guess Ethel and I will die out here by the river, it's peaceful and quiet. We do love it," Dad replied. Slowly Dad pulled into the drive toward our little house. It looked like a mansion to me; I was ready for some home time. Dad walked around to Mrs. Barrett's side of the truck, opened the door and extended his hand to help her out. He then took our bags from the back of the truck and we followed him to the house. I couldn't help myself, I ran around them,

Thanksgiving

jumped on the porch and threw open the front door. "Mother, Mother," I yelled as I raced in. Mother was coming out of the kitchen, drying her hands on her apron. "Kathryn, my darling, I have missed you so much," as we fell into each other's arms hugging and kissing. I was so consumed with greeting my Mother, I totally forgot about Mrs. Barrett. Finally Dad said, "Ethel, Kathryn has a surprise for you." "What?" Just then Mrs. Barrett stepped into the doorway. "Oh, my goodness, Carol Ann Barrett." They ran toward one another and embraced. "I can't believe my eyes. You haven't changed a bit Carol Ann," Mother exclaimed. "Well, neither have you Ethel Collier. I can't wait to hear all about you and what you've been up to since we graduated many years ago. One thing I do know, you and Chris have raised a wonderful daughter. I certainly wish she was mine; I have almost adopted her. I am so glad she is staying with me." "So am I," Mother said with a smile, "you don't know what a comfort it is for Chris and me knowing she is with you."

"Well Kathryn, tell your Dad and me all about your new job, we are so anxious to hear about everything." "Ok Mother, there will be plenty of time for that, where are the boys?" "Oh, they both have new fishing poles and have gone down to the river," Mother told me. "Please excuse me Mrs. Barrett, I must go see my brothers. I'll be back shortly; as I yelled over my shoulder running out the back door." I took my shoes off, so I could feel the cool grass under my feet. I could see them standing on the river bank and I began to

THE RIVER OF LIFE

call to them as I got a bit closer. "Hey, do you care more about fishing than seeing your old long-lost sister?" They turned around, dropped their poles and started running toward me. Brady reached me first and we embraced each other with hugs and kisses. "I have really missed you guys." Now Peter had reached us. He grabbed me around the neck and pretended to throw me to the ground, but he only gave me a bear hug. "Hey sis, you look great, all grown up." So do you both, I told them. It seemed like forever since I had seen them. We slowly walked back to the river bank, they picked up their poles and we stood and looked at the river for a time. I had missed the river almost as much as my family. If I ever had a worry or concern of something, the river gave me peace and comfort.

We finally walked back to the house and entered through the back door. I could smell a great dinner cooking. Mrs. Barrett and Mother were in the kitchen talking so hard they didn't notice us. "What's for dinner Mother?" I made your favorite, Chicken and Dumplings. Yum, yum that sounds great. "My Mother makes the best Chicken and Dumplings in the whole river community," I told Mrs. Barrett. "I'm sure Kathryn, she was always the star cook when we were in High School Home Economics. I knew Ethel would be the best wife and Mother way back then." "You nailed it Mrs. Barrett, she certainly is." I walked over to my Mother, gave her a hug and picked a piece of stewed chicken cooling on the plate. I was starving, I couldn't wait. "What can I do to help you Mother?" "Well, you can set the table. Use our

Thanksgiving

best dishes Kathryn, we have very special guests tonight; Carol Ann and you."

We sat down to dinner and after my Dad gave a beautiful blessing, the wonderful food was enjoyed by everyone. "Mother, you and Mrs. Barrett sit and visit, the boys and I will clean the kitchen. It will give us some time to talk about what's going on." "Let's go sit on the porch," Dad said as he headed for the back-screen door." "That would be wonderful," Mrs. Barrett said, "I do love these cool nights." "Let me grab Carol Ann and me a shawl first Chris," Mother said as she headed for the bedroom. "That's probably a good idea, it is cool, and is such a clear star filled night, I don't want you girls to miss it," Dad stated.

Dad, the boys and I went to bed leaving Mother and Mrs. Barrett to continue their chatting. They must have talked well into the night. When I woke the next morning and stumbled from my room, Mother was already up. I could smell turkey baking and she was peeling potatoes. "What can I do Mother?" "Oh nothing right now dear, I have the cornbread baking for the dressing and 'ole tom' is in the oven. I baked the pies yesterday and made some cranberries and a pea salad. I want to finish these potatoes, and then I am going to prepare us a light breakfast, so we won't starve before dinner is finished." "That's a great idea Mother, Mrs. Barrett and I usually have poached egg, tea and toast." "Good, that's what I'll fix. Carol Ann is still sleeping, we stayed up quite late, I hope she rested well. It's a good thing I had washed the bedding from the boy's bed yesterday. The boys

THE RIVER OF LIFE

slept on a pallet on the living room floor last night, better go wake them before Carol Ann gets up. Tell them to fold the blankets and put them and the pillows on my bed." "Ok Mother," I replied as I went into the living room, reached down and jerked the blanket off the boys. "Hey, stop it sis, don't you have any manners?" they shouted as they both kicked at me and started laughing. "Mother said to fold your bedding and put it and your pillows on her bed, hurry before Mrs. Barrett gets up," I told them. "Ok," they said, as they both slowly got to their feet and started to fold the bedding. I went back in the kitchen to help Mother.

"Where's Dad this morning Mother?" "He's in the barn; one of our milk cows has been poorly and your Dad is keeping a close eye on her." "I'll go out and say hello to both," I responded as I laughed softly and walked out the back door. Dad was standing by the cow gently rubbing her down the length of her back. "What seems to be wrong with her Dad?" "Don't know Kathryn, I first thought she got hold of some bitter weed, but she just seems to move slowly, we haven't been keeping her milk for the last few days. I've been giving her some medicine I got from the Vet in town, so hopefully, she will be better real soon. Guess it is just a virus of some kind." Certainly hope she gets better Dad," I said as I turned to go back into the house. Mother's fixing a light breakfast, so come in soon. "Ok I will," Dad said, as he continued to rub the cows back.

When I got back in the kitchen, Mrs. Barrett had gotten up and was in her robe helping Mother

Thanksgiving

make toast and tea. "Kathryn and I always eat in our robes, hope that is ok," Mrs. Barrett said. "Perfect, I want you to feel at home and comfortable," Mother responded. "Well I certainly do," Mrs. Barrett replied.

We ate our breakfast and Mother continued to work on our Thanksgiving dinner. Mrs. Barrett had gotten dressed and came back into the living room. "Would you like to take a walk down by the river?" I asked. "Oh Kathryn," I would love to see that river of yours." "Great, grab your sweater and we'll be on our way." The boys were playing catch in the front yard and Dad was sitting on the porch relaxing as we prepared to leave for the river. "We'll be back soon," I yelled to my Dad. "Take your time and enjoy it, it's a sight to see, Dad responded." "Oh Kathryn, you were right about the beautiful trees and the river bank," Mrs. Barrett remarked as we arrived at the river. "Well, this is not the prettiest time of the year, the fall leaves are mostly gone now that winter is almost here, I apologetically stated." "Well, it's still lovely, so calm and serene," Mrs. Barrett said. I now know why you aren't in love with the City, this is God's creation. "Correct Mrs. Barrett," only God could pull this off.

Mrs. Barrett and I slowly walked back toward the house. I knew Mother would be about finished with dinner and I wanted to set the table for her. "Ethel, we could smell the dinner almost from the river, it smells divine," Mrs. Barrett said. "I hope you enjoy it; this is one of our favorite times of the year," Mother told her. "Mother, Mrs. Barrett and I were able to pick some of the few remaining

THE RIVER OF LIFE

wild flowers down by the river bank for the dining room table." "Perfect Kathryn, put them in my good vase, that will be lovely." If you want to set the table now Kathryn, that would be great, use your Grandmothers' china and the white linen napkins in the buffet drawer.

The table was ready, and Mother was beginning to finish up all the food. I took the salads from the refrigerator and put the bread in a basket. Dad was carving the turkey and Mrs. Barrett was mashing the potatoes. "Well, Mother said, I think we are ready to sit down and have the blessing." We all six took our seats around the dining room table, joined hands and my Dad said one of his beautiful prayers. After the blessing Dad said, it's Thanksgiving Day and before we eat, let's go around the table and let everyone say what they are thankful for. I'll start. The most important thing I am thankful for is my family and God's protection. The other thing is our milk cow seems to be recovering. Brady snickered at Dad's last thankfulness. Then it was Mother's turn. Well, of course I too am thankful for my family, and I'm also thankful Kathryn and Carol Ann are here with us. Then Mrs. Barrett said, I am thankful Ethel wrote to me requesting our lovely Kathryn stay with me. I'm thankful for my and Kathryn's friendship, and thankful Kathryn wouldn't hush until I said I would come home with her for Thanksgiving, and I am so thankful I did. Then it was Peter's turn. Well, he said slowly, I'm thankful I made the basketball team in my first year of High School, and thankful Sissy came home for Thanksgiving. Finally it was my little brother Brady

Thanksgiving

turn. Well, he said as he looked toward the ceiling with one eye closed, I am thankful Sissy and Mrs. Barrett came for Thanksgiving.

Finally, it was my turn. I have so many things to be thankful for, dinner would be cold if I said all of them. So, I will just say a few. I am thankful for Mrs. Barrett, for my family, for my new job, for new friends and especially for God's protection while our family was apart.

"Amen to all those thanks," Dad said, let's eat!

After dinner the food put away, the dishes washed and put back in the buffet; we all settled down in the living room to relax and chat. Soon it was evening, we snacked a bit then all retired to bed.

Friday and Saturday were spent just relaxing and visiting. Mother and Mrs. Barrett continued to reminisce about their youthful years. Sunday morning arrived and we all went to our little Church. I couldn't wait to see Miss Hattie and introduce her to Mrs. Barrett. I also wanted to tell her about my new job. When we pulled up to the Church, I saw Miss Hattie getting out of her car. "Miss Hattie" I called, "wait up. I want you to meet someone," as I stepped over the tailgate of the truck onto the bumper. She turned and started toward me with open arms. "Kathryn, I am so glad to see you." "I have a job, Miss Hattie; I am working as a steno/typist in a Law Firm." "Oh Kathryn, I am so happy, I knew you would be able to get a good job, do you like it?" "I love it, the two Attorneys' I work for are such nice gentlemen and the work is very interesting." "Miss Hattie, I want you to meet Mrs.

THE RIVER OF LIFE

Barrett, I am staying with her in the city and guess what, she and my Mother were childhood friends. "Well I'll say," Miss Hattie said, "small world. I am so glad to meet you Mrs. Barrett, call me Hattie." "Call me Carol Ann," Mrs. Barrett said as they gently shook hands. We all went into the Church and what a wonderful feeling came over me. There is just something special about that little Country Church that other Churches can't compare with. The service was wonderful; Mrs. Barrett really enjoyed it too.

When we arrived back home, Mother prepared a light lunch while Mrs. Barrett and I got our things together, it would soon be time for Dad to take us back to the bus station. We ate, visited for a bit longer and soon it was time to leave. I had been dreading leaving from the time we arrived on Wednesday afternoon, but I knew we must return to the city.

I kissed my little brothers and gave them 'be good instructions,' mind Mother and Dad and study real hard. Then, I turned toward Mother. My eyes were already beginning to well up with tears. "Oh my darling, don't be sad," Mother said. "Christmas will be here before you know it and we'll be together again." She held me tight for several seconds, kissing my neck and stroking my long hair. "I love you so much Kathryn Collier and I am so proud of you." "I love you too Mother, and I will write you often."

That reminds me, Mrs. Barrett said. I want to leave my telephone number, and if you ever need to get a message to Kathryn, you can reach us at

Thanksgiving

this number. Mrs. Barrett pulled a piece of paper from her hand bag and begin to scratch some numbers on it. Mother and Dad still did not have a telephone but would have one as soon as the Telephone Company had finally run lines out to the people living on the river bank. Since they had electricity; Dad had a well drilled for running water. If they only had a telephone that would be great, but in time I guess they would get one.

I had saved my goodbyes for Dad until we reached the bus station. He got out of the truck and came around to Mrs. Barrett's side, opened the truck door and extended his hand to help her out of the truck. I jumped out behind her as Dad was getting our bags from the back of the truck. "Well, Carol Ann, it has been a real pleasure having you visit us," Dad said. "I just want you to know how grateful Ethel and I are for taking in our little girl." "My pleasure, I assure you Chris, she is a real comfort and joy to have around," Mrs. Barrett responded. "Thanks so much for such a wonderful holiday in your home and making me feel like one of the family. It was so good getting to see my old friend Ethel and talk about old times." "Come home with Kathryn anytime, you are more than welcome," Dad replied. Now it was time to tell my Dad goodbye. Just as before, I began to tear up as I started toward him. "Hey, what is this? You're a big girl" he said trying to take light of my tears, as he reached for me and hugged me tightly. "You will always be our little girl, no matter how old you get." "Thanks Dad, I love you so much." "I love you too sweetie," as he picked up our bags and

THE RIVER OF LIFE

we headed for the bus station. He waited until the bus pulled into the station and we were boarded. Then, he turned and walked toward the truck. Our holiday was over, but it had been wonderful.

Chapter 15

My Job, On My Own

Monday morning came, and my excitement was soaring. This would be my first day at my job without Emily. I was nervous but confident. I had taken good notes and Emily was thrilled with my training. I arrived early, put my things away and was ready when I heard Mr. Davis come out of his office. "Well good morning Kathryn, how was your holiday?" "Wonderful Mr. Davis, I went home and spent it with my family." "Great, so did I" he said, as he crossed his arm and leaned against the filing cabinet. "My parents live just a few miles out of the city and my two younger sisters were home from college, so it was a wonderful family reunion. We had too much food though, my Mother is a wonderful cook, she just cooks too much of it, but the left overs are great," he said. "Well Kathryn, if you want to grab your pad and pencil, we will get started. We'll meet in the conference room as soon as Curtis gets off the phone. Feel free to grab yourself a cup of coffee or tea if you like. Curtis and I can't function without our morning coffee,"

THE RIVER OF LIFE

he said with a smile, as he headed toward the conference room.

Our morning session went well. I had taken all the notes from all the client cases and returned to my desk to start typing them. This is going to be such an interesting job, I'm going to love it, I thought. After all the notes were typed, filed in the client's folders and put away, it was time for lunch. I again walked across the street to the little park. It was almost too chilly, but I had my winter coat and the freshness of the winter air felt good. It won't be long though before I will need to just eat my lunch in the office. We have a small lunch area behind the conference room with table, chairs, refrigerator, coffee pot and a hot plate for making tea, so it was a wonderful arrangement. I just wanted to get out of the office this morning as I knew it would probably be my last day in the park until spring.

Chapter 16

Christmas Holiday

The weeks rolled by and it was time to go home for Christmas. I had bought a few things for Mother, Dad and my brothers with what I had left after paying Mrs. Barrett my rent. "Now Kathryn, if this will run you short on your Christmas shopping," Mrs. Barrett said, as she held up the money I had placed in her hand; "you can pay me later." "Nonsense Mrs. Barrett, I have budgeted for my Christmas shopping. Are you sure you won't join me and my family for Christmas?" "No, but thank you, I had a note from my sister and she and her daughter are coming here for Christmas," Mrs. Barrett said. It will be her first Christmas since she lost her husband and she is feeling lonely, so I'm glad they will be here, maybe I can cheer them up. "That sounds nice Mrs. Barrett, maybe another time," I replied. "Sure," she said, as she turned toward the kitchen. But for now, we must eat supper; I'll have it ready in a minute. How does chicken salad and some fresh fruit sound? 'Great,' I said as she walked away.

THE RIVER OF LIFE

I boarded the bus with my small bag and the few gifts I had for the family, and I was on my way home. It would be good to see my family again although it had only been four weeks since I was home for Thanksgiving. I was ready for another visit. I probably wouldn't be going back home again until Easter, which would be my longest time without seeing my family, but I was adjusting to being away.

Christmas holiday was wonderful, and I returned to Mrs. Barrett's and back to work. The New Year celebration had come and gone. Emily's baby girl was born on January 10th; who they named Ruby, weighing 7 lbs. 11 oz's. Emily's husband Tim, called the office to let us know the good news. Everything went well and both Emily and baby were doing great. She would be going home from the hospital in a few days and I made plans to visit her.

Chapter 17

Miss Hattie's Death

The weeks and months seemed to flash by and now it was 1947. I focused on my job and helping Mrs. Barrett with the marketing, cooking and cleaning. I had been working at the Law Firm for four years now, Peter had graduated from High School, and Duke was 16 in the 10th grade. Mother and Dad were doing well, just a few winter colds, but otherwise good. The phone company had finally attached the phone wires to the electrical poles which gave the families living on the river bank phone access. Thank goodness! Although, I didn't call too often, I knew if I needed to reach my folks, I could.

One Friday summer evening, Mrs. Barrett and I were sitting on the porch enjoying the cool breeze when her phone rang. She rose slowly and made her way into the house to answer it. In a few seconds, I heard her say, "Kathryn, the phone is for you, it's your Father." I was joyful for a second, and then a wave of fear overcame me. Was Dad just calling to say hello or was there something wrong?

THE RIVER OF LIFE

I raced to the phone taking it from Mrs. Barrett hand. "Hello," I said in a questioning voice. "Hi Sweetheart, my Dad's voice came back saying. I have a bit of bad news." "What?" "What is it Dad?" Well, they found Miss Hattie this morning and she had passed away sitting in her chair with her book in her lap. I knew you'd want to know. Oh no, I cried uncontrollably, not Miss Hattie! How can I get along without my dear sweet Miss Hattie? "I know," my Dad said in a consoling voice, she didn't suffer Sweetheart. "They said she couldn't have looked more peaceful and happier. Will you want to come home Kathryn?" "Yes Dad, I replied. When is the service?" "It's going to be Sunday afternoon at 2:00 p.m. Kathryn, when you have your bus schedule, ring me back and I will pick you up when you arrive." "Ok Dad, this is so sad, I will miss her so much". We all will Kathryn, just try to focus on the good times and all the great things Miss Hattie did for our little river community. "I know, I'll try. I'll call you back shortly."

I called the bus station and found they had a bus leaving the city at 7:45 a.m. Saturday morning arriving in our town at 8:55 a.m. I called my Dad back and gave him the information. I packed my best dress and good slippers for the service, along with something to wear to the viewing. The bus ride gave me time to think about Miss Hattie and what an impact she had made on so many of the kids she had taught. Some of her students were grown now with grandchildren. She had retired at the end of the school year right after I moved to

Miss Hattie's Death

the city. I was so glad Mrs. Barrett had a chance to meet Miss Hattie, if only for a few minutes.

My bus pulled into the station right on time Saturday morning and I could already see my Dad. I grabbed my bag, exited the bus, and walked toward him. He was already heading my way. He took my bag from me and hugged me tight. "I'm so sorry sweetheart; I know you and Miss Hattie had a special bond." "We did Dad, very special."

Mother had fixed breakfast when we arrived home; she too was trying hard to console me. Both of my brothers were very upset also. We ate our breakfast, and Mother and I sat in the living room and reminisced about Miss Hattie. I went to my room, laid on the bed and rested a bit, as the visitation would start at 6:00 p.m.

We got in the truck and started into town to the Funeral Home for the viewing. When we arrived and entered the Funeral Home, we saw so many beautiful flowers surrounding the casket. Miss Hattie would have been so pleased. She loved flowers. There was a line of several of my classmates waiting to sign the memorial book, and while we stood in line, we chatted softly about the great memories we each held dear about Miss Hattie. When we reached the casket, there she was in her navy-blue dress with the lace gently placed on the white collar and cuffs. She looked peaceful. I knew why, she was with Jesus.

Sunday morning after breakfast, we went to Church. It was good seeing everyone but there was a sadness among the congregation. Miss Hattie's normal seat was empty. I thought it reverent of

THE RIVER OF LIFE

everyone not to sit in Miss Hattie's seat, third pew, from the front on the right side. She would have found humor in that. After Church, we went back home for lunch. Mother had gotten up early and fried chicken and made potato salad so we could eat quickly and get to the Funeral Home in town by 2:00 p.m. I had packed my bag before Church since my bus left at 5:00 p.m. There would be no reason for Dad to drive me back again after the funeral. The service was a great tribute to a wonderful Christian woman who had been such an asset to our little town.

After driving back from the Cemetery, we went straight to the bus station and sat out front on a bench waiting for my bus to pull in. At 5:00 p.m. sharp it arrived. I kissed my folks and brothers and boarded the bus for Mrs. Barrett's house.

I was thinking about Peter on my way back to the city. Peter was still trying to decide since he graduated whether to get a job in the city or join the Army. He was leaning toward Army, although I didn't want him to, there was talk of the Korean war.

Chapter 18

The Law Firm

Monday morning, and I was back to work at the Law Firm. Mr. Davis and Mr. Simmons hired a lady a bit older than I to be a receptionist. She was very personable and pleasant. She was quiet and did her job. Her name was Helen. She and I seemed to have a connection right away. I was kept busy taking the client file notes and transcribing them. I also had started reading the complete files of the clients I knew would be discussed in the conference room each morning. I wanted to be familiar with the situation. A couple of times, I had reminded either Mr. Davis or Mr. Simmons of facts they had failed to include. They seemed impressed. "Well," Mr. Davis said, guess we're going to have to take you to Court with us so you can hear first-hand what goes on." "Are you serious," I asked. "That would be wonderful Mr. Davis, I would love that!" "Yes indeed, I think you are ready, and you will be a real asset helping us with our cases," he replied. So now my position was to keep the Court dates on my calendar and

THE RIVER OF LIFE

to pull the cases we would try on each Court day. I had carefully gone over each client's file to make sure everything was in the file and in order. I had read them over a couple of times, so I felt ready on the first day we all three went to the Courthouse.

My life was full of the excitement of my new position in the Law Firm. I had a bit more responsibility now and I was enjoying it and taking it very serious. I had been working for Mr. Davis and Mr. Simmons for five years. One late afternoon I was still going over some files for the next day when Mr. Davis walked in. "Kathryn why are you still here?" he asked. "Oh hi Mr. Davis, I wanted to go over the cases we will be taking to Court in the morning to make sure everything is in order," I replied. "Well, it's getting dinner time, how about let's grabbing a bite together and discuss what we have coming up?" "Oh, I don't know Mr. Davis, Mrs. Barrett will be expecting me home." "Well, give her a call, I'm sure she won't mind your eating in the city." "Ok," I said hesitantly. I had never been in a personal position with either Mr. Davis or Mr. Simmons, but I guessed it would be ok. Mrs. Barrett was fine with the arrangement and said, have a nice dinner and she would see me when I got home.

Mr. Davis and I went to a nice restaurant for dinner. We had walked from the office to the restaurant. Mr. Davis and Mr. Simmons parked their cars behind the Law Office. As we walked, Mr. Davis said, "well Kathryn, how long have you been working for Curtis and me?" "Five years sir," I said. "I think it's about time you call me Jonathan or just Jon, what do you think?" "I don't know Mr. Davis,

The Law Firm

I guess I could, it will be strange though." "Good, now that we have that worked out, let's talk about some of those cases," he replied. We were seated at a table in a corner. "This is good, maybe we can talk without too much interruption," Mr. Davis said.

Jon and I had a delicious dinner and great conversation. I was surprised at the ease he had put me in. We finished dinner and it was time to go home. "I'll catch my bus from that corner," I said, as I pointed across the street. "Nonsense Kathryn, I go right by Mrs. Barrett's on my way home, I'll drop you off." Mr. Davis had a small apartment further out of the city. I had heard he and Mr. Simmons talking about where they lived. Mr. Simmons lived with his elderly Mother in the opposite direction of the Law Office.

The next morning, I was anxious to get to work and pack the files in the large leather box on wheels. Mr. Davis was already at the office making the morning coffee he and Mr. Simmons had to have before they could start their day. I had already had my usual breakfast with Mrs. Barrett, I only drink tea. "I don't know how you get started Kathryn," Mr. Davis said, without a couple cups of good ole strong coffee. I laughed shyly. "I know, that's a strange one isn't it?" I said smiling at him. I was beginning to look at Mr. Davis differently since last night. I'm not sure if that's good. Anyway, I didn't feel nervous around him at all anymore. I still wanted to maintain our work relationship, no matter how close friends we became. Mr. Simmons arrived as we were finishing packing up. "Well, boys and girls," Mr. Simmons said with a deep laugh, "let's go get 'em." "I certainly hope so," Mr. Davis said. "We have a couple of difficult cases this morning." "We're very prepared," I said laughing softly. "It looks like Kathryn's more confident than we are," Mr. Simmons said as he gave me a funny wink. "I'll let Helen know we are leaving now," I told the two attorneys over my shoulder, as I walked from Mr. Davis office. Mr. Davis picked up the rolling leather file box and headed out the back where their cars were parked. I'm right behind you, turning to Helen I said, "have a good day; see you tomorrow," as I closed the back door.

The weeks and months passed quickly, and I loved my job with Jon and Curtis. They had continued to include me in all the cases, and I was working more as an assistant rather than an office secretary. They had hired another girl in the front office to help Helen with the filing and appointments. The Law Firm was growing rapidly, and more time was spent at the office by all of us. Jon and I had begun to officially date, having dinner and going to the Light Civic Opera here in the city, at least twice a month. We enjoyed being together and found we had many of the same likes and dislikes. Jon had wanted to meet my family, but I was not ready to take that step. I knew once he met them, our relationship would go to the next level. I was falling in love with Jon. My heart seemed to beat a little faster when he would brush by my shoulder or touch my hand when I handed him a file. I noticed I became flushed when we looked into each other's eyes.

The Law Firm

However, I still needed a bit more time to get to know him. I had now worked at the Law Office for seven years. I was 25 and Jon was 33.

Chapter 19

Peter in The Army

Peter had joined the army and was stationed in Korea. My parents were very anxious about his safety as many of the young soldiers had lost their lives fighting for our Country. Peter and I wrote each other weekly and I knew from his letters, he was scared but wouldn't let the folks know of his fear. He was in a ground platoon and fighting close to the front lines. Although he expressed his fear, he was a dedicated soldier and was there to do his part. He had made many close friends, as Peter explained; you become close when you lay in a fox hole next to each other with live ammo flying over your head. Peter had told me of one close buddy of his whose name was Bill. He and Bill had shared many stories about their families, and what they wanted to do when they were able to get back home. They also talked about one other very important subject. Peter had shared his love for the Lord many times with Bill, however, Bill never responded back with much interest. One night as they lay in the fox hole in the chill of the very dark night, Bill began to ask Peter more questions about his God. Peter pulled his small Bible from his pocket and holding his flashlight with the other hand began to share God's Word with Bill. Bill asked Peter what he needed to do to be a child of God and after Peter read several passages from his Bible to Bill, and praying the sinner's prayer with him, Peter heard Bill's confession. They held each other as Bill wept tears of joy and Peter wept with him, knowing Bill had accepted the Lord with all his heart. When I received the letter from Peter about Bill's new-found salvation, I was thrilled with Peter's persistence to bring Bill to the Lord. In the letters that were to follow weeks later, they continued to share about God's love for them.

Brady was now 19 and attending college out of state. He was a sophomore and doing very well with his studies and making lots of friends. Brady was a very social kid, and everyone seemed to like him instantly. I also corresponded with Brady but not as often as with Peter. I guess he was just too busy to write his big sister much. Brady wanted to be a doctor, so he was taking a lot of classes toward his goal profession. He would have another two years in college, then 4 years in med school, and 2 years in primary practice. He was very excited about his career goals and I was happy he had decided about his future.

The folks were still living by the river and doing well. The last time I had gone home for a visit, my Mother seemed to be slowing down a bit. It scared me a little as she was always so busy with the house, the garden and all the other things she did

Peter in The Army

to keep life going. However, when I questioned her about her health, she threw back her head and laughed, "Oh Kathryn my darling, it's only old age. You forget your Dad and I aren't getting any younger," she said as she continued to wash the dishes and giggle softly.

Chapter 20

Mrs. Barrett's Illness

Winter has finally passed, and spring was upon us. I always loved the spring with the birds singing and preparing for nest building, and all the flowers which just seemed to pop up out of nowhere. Mrs. Barrett's garden was just that paradise. She and I would sit on the back porch and enjoy watching the birds carrying pieces of dried grass, feathers and sticks while they busily built their nest. Mrs. Barrett had not been feeling well and had made several trips to the Dr. but had said little about the test results. One evening while we were enjoying the summer breeze and watching the sun slowly fall below the horizon, Mrs. Barrett said to me, "Kathryn, I have something to tell you, Mrs. Barrett said in a soft low voice. The Dr. seems to think I have some type of blood disease. They are not sure if it is cancer or not, they are still running tests. I wanted you to know first and if I become too ill to function, I'm sure my sister will stay with me. She's alone now since she lost her husband and her daughter married

THE RIVER OF LIFE

a few years ago and moved out of state. It would be a good time for both of us to spend some time together while I am recovering." My heart sank as I listened intently to Mrs. Barrett's words. "Mrs. Barrett, I'm sure Jon and Curtis would allow me to take time off if I needed to stay home with you anytime. They are very good about things like that." "Oh no Kathryn, I'm sure I will be fine and like I said, I know my sister would welcome a visit," she replied. We'll wait and see what the final test result shows. We continued to watch the sunset without speaking anymore of Mrs. Barrett's condition.

Chapter 21

My Feelings for Jon

Summer was quickly upon us and the girls in the front office were planning their vacations. "Kathryn, when do you plan to take your vacation this year?" Jon asked. "I don't know, Jon. I thought perhaps around Memorial Day if no one else takes that week." "Well, how about if I take my vacation that week too and we visit your folks?" I jerked around to look at him as he was smiling and gave me a wink. "Well Miss Collier, what about it?" I had put Jon off for several months about meeting the folks, but now he was beginning to pressure me. I knew I was deeply in love with Jon. I just didn't know if this would be rushing our relationship. "Ok," I said, I will check with my folks and make sure they don't have plans for that week and let you know. "Well," Jon said as he handed me a pencil. "Miss Collier pencil me in on the office calendar. I plan to be visiting your folks on Memorial Day week."

I had contacted Mother and Dad and gave them the news; I would be bringing Jon home with me. I had told them about him but had not indicated the seriousness of our relationship. I guess now they would know my feelings for him. I truly loved Jon and could see myself marrying him and raising a family. Our work relationship had not changed too much, however, once we took it to the next level, I'm sure things would seem different. For that reason, I continued to hold back. Jon is such an understanding man, I'm sure he will make things easy and comfortable for me.

Our travel plans were made. Jon would pick me up Friday evening around 6:00 p.m. and we would drive to my folk's home. Our plan was to stay until Tuesday and return to the city on Tuesday afternoon. I wanted to return as Mrs. Barrett would be taking her first treatment on Thursday. They found she had a type of Lymphoma. From all tests, it was considered very treatable.

Jon and I arrived at my folk's house Friday evening around 8:30 p.m. I had told Mother not to prepare dinner for us, we planned to stop on the way and grab a bite. When we turned up the drive, everything looked beautiful. It was just getting dusky dark; we could see the yard. It was in full bloom and the grass never looked better. The moon was bright, the sky was clear and full of stars. I glanced down toward the river and could see the water sparkling in the moonlight. I couldn't wait until morning to show the river to Jon. We walked upon the porch and Dad was already opening the door. I ran in front of Jon and hugged my Dad. Once I let go of him, he looked at Jon and said, "Well, guess this is the young man we

My Feelings for Jon

have been hearing so much about." Jon extended his hand and gave that good firm attorney handshake. "So glad to finally meet you, Mr. Collier." "Call me Chris," Dad said with a big smile. By this time, Mother had come from the kitchen to get in on the greeting. I ran to her and embraced her like I was still twelve, then quickly introduced her to Jon. She extended her arms around his neck and said, "welcome Jon, we are so happy to finally meet you." "Me too. I have been begging Kathryn for this visit for months." Jon replied as they all laughed. "Oh stop it," (slightly embarrassed,) I said with a shy smile.

Mother had turned the boy's bedroom into a very comfortable guest room. She had white linens on the bed. On the bedside table she had a summer bouquet, reading lamp and a couple of good books. She had gone to a lot of trouble for our visit and I was very proud of her for making us feel so special. We had sat on the porch for a while after we arrived, watching the lightning bugs and listening to the crickets. It was so peaceful compared to the City. Jon was not used to the quietness of the country and seemed to really enjoy it. After we said goodnight, we retired to our rooms. Mother had put pink rosebud linens on my bed, and I too had a bouquet of flowers. As I lay down in my bed, I couldn't believe I was old enough to bring a man home to my parent's house for the night. I snickered to myself and felt great joy and love for the man who was sleeping in the next room.

Morning came, and I was awakened by the aroma of fresh brewed coffee and frying bacon.

THE RIVER OF LIFE

My Mother had always prepared a large breakfast when we were kids and still did for herself and Dad. Jon certainly was pleased when he emerged from his room all showered, shaved and dressed to see what a huge breakfast Mother was preparing. Jon usually had strong coffee and sometimes a chocolate donut. He looked so handsome. I loved him dressed in his casual clothes, they make him look young and sexy. I really did love this guy. When we were at work, I tried to focus on business, but when away from the office, my heart ached for him and his affection. I just hope Mother and Dad would love him as much as I did. Of course, I knew it would take time. Jon and I planned to take our courtship slow as we both had plenty of time. I wanted him to be able to concentrate on the Law Firm and build his business and I would like to work beside him, helping him build it.

After breakfast, I was so excited to finally show Jon the river. We grabbed a blanket from the bench on the back porch and walked toward the river bank. The sky was the bluest, and the trees were beautiful shades of dark green, as they slowly swayed in the morning air. The wild flowers were in full bloom in shades of yellows and pinks. Jon was taken by the beauty of the area and the fresh smell of the morning air. We walked up to the river bank and watched the water move slowly down stream, as if it was a bit sleepy, trying to wake for our arrival. The birds were fluttering back and forth from tree to tree and singing as they went. "The river and I have had this love affair since I was a young child. I can't explain it, I told him. I just

My Feelings for Jon

get this peaceful, happy feeling when I watch the river flow downstream." "I can see what you mean Kathryn. It does give a sense of peace."

Jon unfolded the blanket and spread it in the shade of the beautiful maple tree. We sat close to each other in the quiet of the morning. Jon was holding my hand. We didn't speak, just enjoyed the closeness of each other. Finally, we got up, picked up the blanket, folded it, and slowly started toward the house. We had only taken a few steps when Jon holding my hand tightly, stopped me, turned me toward him, lifted my chin to his and tenderly kissed me. We stood embraced for some time, and then he put his hands around my face, looking me straight in the eyes and said, "Kathryn Collier, I Love you with all my heart. I am so happy and content when I am near you. I have never felt this way about anyone else in my life." I knew I loved Jon too, I just had to get the nerve to say it. Suddenly without warning, I looked into his eyes, put my hand on his cheek and softly said, "I love you too, Jon." We embraced again and held each other tight for several seconds before continuing to walk toward my folk's house. As we walked my thoughts focused on what had just happened. We had expressed our love for each other by my beloved river and under the beautiful maple tree, what could be more perfect? My heart was filled with joy as we continued walking without saying anything more. We both knew in our hearts; this was real for both of us.

The rest of our visit with my folks was very relaxing and peaceful. We took several more

THE RIVER OF LIFE

walks down by the river before packing up Jon's car and heading back to the city. I had enjoyed our visit with my folks more than I had ever imagined. I was so at ease and relaxed, I surprised myself. For the first time when it was time to leave my parents, I didn't cry like a 12-year-old child. Suddenly, I realized I had transferred some of my love and affection to my beloved Jon. Of course, I still love my parents the same, but I realized I had grown up over the past few days. I felt full and content as Jon's car turned from the driveway and headed toward the City. No longer did my heart ache for my parents. I had turned a corner in my life and was happy I had turned it with Jon.

Chapter 22

Mrs. Barrett's Cancer

When we arrived back at Mrs. Barrett's house, she was sitting on the porch. The way the light hit her face, she looked pale and drawn. That scared me, I had never noticed her looking this pale. She got up from her chair when we stopped in front of the house and greeted both Jon and me. "How are you today Mrs. Barrett?" Jon lovingly asked her. "Oh, doing ok Jon, how was your visit with Ethel and Chris?" "Wonderful," he responded as he looked at me with a secret wink. We had a great visit and I finally saw Kathryn's river. "Well, what did you think of it?" Mrs. Barrett asked. It was all Kathryn said and more Jon responded. It's very peaceful and comforting just sitting and watching the water move slowly as if telling you to relax and enjoy. Jon reached for me and gave me a tight squeeze around my shoulders.

"Well girls, guess I had better get on home, Jon remarked. I have a bit of paper work to do before I go into the office tomorrow. Kathryn, you enjoy the rest of your vacation."

THE RIVER OF LIFE

"I was wondering if I could take you and Mrs. Barrett to dinner in the next couple of nights? You girls talk it over and let me know when and where you would like to go. But for now, just sit out here on the porch and enjoy the beauty of this lovely garden." Jon took my hand and gently kissed my cheek before stepping from the porch, turned and gave a wave as he got into his car. "He's a wonderful young man Kathryn, I think he's a keeper." I smiled thinking to myself, you are so right Mrs. Barrett, he's a keeper.

Thursday morning Mrs. Barrett and I went to the clinic for her first treatment. It would take approximately 3 1/2 hours so I had grabbed a book to read while I waited in the adjourning area. I had spoken with the nurse after Mrs. Barrett was hooked up to the IV, about what we should expect in the next few days. She explained the treatment was light since they felt the cancer had been caught in the early stages. In fact, they said Mrs. Barrett would probably not lose her hair. She may feel tired for the next few days, and then she would be back to normal. I was pleased to hear she would not be deathly ill. The time went by quickly. After the treatment was finished it was nearly noon and I suggested we stop and get some lunch before going home. Mrs. Barrett agreed. She thought lunch might help her feel a bit stronger. After eating and relaxing for a time, we returned home. Mrs. Barrett went into her room and laid down to rest. I went onto the porch and dialed Jon's office. Helen answered the phone and when I asked to speak to Jon, she seemed a bit confused that I would call my boss while I was on vacation. It looks like we will soon have to tell the girls in the front office about my and Jon's relationship. Suddenly, Jon was on the phone saying hello, hello? My thoughts were so consumed with what Helen must be thinking, I didn't realize Jon had answered. "Oh, I said quickly, how are you doing?" this is Kathryn. Jon laughing said, "I know who you are. Did you think I would forget you so quickly?" "No, I responded, I just wanted to see how things were going at the office." "Oh, come on Kathryn," Jon chuckled, "you just wanted to hear my voice, right?" "Sure, Sure" I teasingly said, "I can't live without you." "Well, Miss Collier, my feelings exactly. When can we have dinner?" "Mrs. Barrett said she thought she would feel fine if we had dinner tomorrow night," I responded. However, if she is not feeling well, I will call you and make dinner here. I'll let you know tomorrow for sure.

"The treatment she had today seemed to go well. Mrs. Barrett is now lying down, and she is not expected to become too ill. Mrs. Barrett has been healthy most of her life, so being sick will be different for her. "As you know, I told Jon, Mrs. Barrett and her husband never had children. I'm sure she would have loved to have a family. I know she would have been a wonderful mother." "You're right Kathryn, she seemed like a sweet, gentle woman."

"I will wait to hear from you tomorrow to finalize our dinner plans. I miss seeing you at the office but relax and enjoy your time off. I have a lot of work piling up for you when Monday comes," Jon said

THE RIVER OF LIFE

as he gave a deep joking laugh. "Ok I said, talk to you tomorrow." Just before we hung up Jon whispered, "I love you Kathryn," "I love you too Jon".

Friday morning Mrs. Barrett seemed to sleep in a little longer than usual. I had made the tea and was waiting to make the toast until I heard her stirring. Finally, she came into the kitchen. She looked unusually tired. "Did you sleep well," I asked her? "I seemed to sleep, I just don't feel rested", she responded. "How about a poached egg with your toast and tea this morning," I asked? I think you need extra nourishment. "Ok" she said, as I continued to prepare our breakfast. Later in the morning, I found Mrs. Barrett lying on the couch still looking exhausted. I'm going to call Jon and tell him I will fix dinner here tonight. Oh no Kathryn, I don't want to spoil the plan. You and Jon go ahead and have a nice dinner together. Nonsense, I'm going to make us a big pot of my Mothers' chicken soup. Jon will love it and a nice hot bowl of it will make you feel better. We'll have some cornbread to go with it. I'll call Jon right now and tell him. "Oh Kathryn," she was saying as I walked away. "I'm not listening Mrs. Barrett; I'm making soup and that's final."

Jon arrived after work. He had gone home and changed into his shorts and knit shirt. "Hope I'm not dressed too casual for dinner with two beautiful ladies," he said as he jumped upon the porch where Mrs. Barrett and I was sitting. "You look wonderful Jon. I'm just sorry I have spoiled your and Kathryn's plans." "Our plan is not spoiled, she has cooked dinner, hasn't she?" Jon said as he looked

Mrs. Barrett's Cancer

at me and gave that cute little wink. "Well sure she cooked, and I know it will be delicious, but I don't want to be a burden," Mrs. Barrett responded. "Nonsense, I chimed in." You of all people could never be a burden." Jon, how about a glass of cool lemonade while the cornbread is finish baking? That sounds wonderful Kathryn. Would you like another glass Mrs. Barrett? Oh no, I don't want to be too full, so I can enjoy that wonderful soup and cornbread.

Chapter 23

Bill's Death

Monday morning and I was back to work. Not only did I enjoy my job, but always excited to be near Jon. My love for him was continuing to grow with each passing day. Monday's always went by so quickly, as we were so busy with weekend mail etc.

When I returned home, there was a letter from Peter. I was excited when I saw it on the table in the front hall. I grabbed my mail, shouted hello to Mrs. Barrett and went to my room to change my clothes and read Bill's letter. I tore it open with excitement and began to read as follows:

Dear Sis:

My hand can barely move as I write this letter. My dear friend Bill was killed in action yesterday. We were able to get him to the Medic Hospital, but he was too injured and there wasn't anything they could do. I held his hand and was able to Pray with him and he was able to say goodbye to me. Kathryn, my heart is breaking, I can hardly breathe. Now I know what it means to have a broken heart. The Sergeant said his parents would be getting the news today and I can't take my mind off them. I can only imagine how broken hearted they will be. I have never really feared battle until yesterday, and today, I'm scared to death. I can't wait until I can come home for good. I didn't write the folks about Bill, I don't want them to be more worried about me. I will wait until I come home to tell them.

Well Sis, sorry to send such bad news. The good news is, Bill is with the Lord. I am so thankful Bill accepted Him and now will be in Heaven. Pray for me Sis. Pray I can accept Bill's death and continue with my duty as a soldier. I am here to protect our Country and want to do my part.

I love you with all my heart, Kathryn.
Peter.

After reading Peter's letter, I wept and prayed for Peter's safety. I gave praise to God that Bill is with Him and no longer in fear of war and death. Death of a loved one is so traumatic, we don't understand it, but we must rely on our faith and know God is in charge and He has a plan for our lives.

Bill's Death

Summer quickly flew by and fall was upon us. The leaves were falling, and the days were getting chilly. Peter and I had continued to correspond weekly. In his last letter, he had the greatest news, he will be home for Christmas. I am looking forward to his homecoming and meeting Jon. Jon and I plan to visit the folks over the Christmas holiday. Brady will be home from college as well. It will be a great time of celebration.

Mrs. Barrett finished her treatments and was doing well. Her sister came and stayed with us for four weeks during the treatments. It was good having her as I knew Mrs. Barrett would be well cared for while I was at work. She would have good meals and someone to visit with her.

Chapter 24

Christmas & The Proposal

I had started my Christmas shopping right after Thanksgiving and was finished two weeks before Christmas. It seemed the weeks and months flew by and it would be time to go visit the folks in 10 days. I was getting very excited to see my family. Peter would arrive two days before Jon and me, and Brady was scheduled to get home two days before Peter. I knew my Mother was cooking up a storm and getting excited to have us all home. Finally, all the gifts were wrapped, the car packed, and we were on our way. We had left the City a bit early to beat the traffic. We had stopped and had a nice dinner and tried to relax for a bit before continuing.

It was around 8:00 p.m. when we pulled up the dirt road leading to my parent's home. As usual. I glanced over toward the river and could see its' sparkling water. The leaves had fallen so it was very visible from the folk's driveway. When we arrived, Peter and Brady's cars were both there. I couldn't get out of Jon's car fast enough. "I'll get the luggage," Jon laughingly said. I totally missed the steps and jumped upon the porch. When I opened the screen, Peter had opened the door and we both grabbed each other in a tight embrace. He looked much older and more muscular. He had turned into a man while in Korea. He looked tired, but otherwise great. We continued to hold each other when suddenly a voice said, "hey, what about me? Don't you care about your baby brother anymore?" I turned loose of Peter, grabbed Brady, and attempted to put him in a head lock. He twisted my arm laughing and said, "guess you can't handle me like you used to." I willingly gave in to him and kissed him uncontrollably. That's enough he yelled. Mom make her stop!

Jon was making his way in with the luggage. Peter ran to help him. "You must be Jon," Peter said, and "You must be Peter," Jon said with a hand shake and a big hug. "I'm happy to finally meet you Jon. I have heard a lot about you, more than I probably should know," Peter laughed as he hit Jon on the back. After a lot of hugging, laughing and talking, we all went to bed. I lay down but couldn't go to sleep; there had been just too much wonderful excitement. I picked up a book Mother had so lovingly place on my bedside table and began to read. Before long, I was asleep with the light on and the book on my chest.

The next morning when I woke, and came from my room, I saw Dad and Jon on the porch talking. They seemed totally engrossed in conversation. I opened the door and told them breakfast was almost ready. "Aren't you guys cold?" I asked, as

Christmas & The Proposal

I smiled and closed the door. In a few minutes they were seated, and Mother was sitting the food on the table. Jon loved my Mother's breakfast food; he never gets that at home. After breakfast, Jon hugged me and said, "hey, when you get dressed, would you like to visit that river of yours?" "Certainly, you know I can't wait to go say hello." We got our jackets and walked down the dirt road toward the river. Jon had grabbed a blanket and a couple of folded lawn chairs from the porch. He sat the chairs under the most beautiful maple tree in the world. Its branches were bare, but the way they extended toward the river was totally beautiful. We sat down, and Jon covered us both with the blanket. "Well Miss Collier, are you happy to be home?" Jon asked. I am so happy Jon, seeing my brothers and parents makes me the happiest person in the world.

"Kathryn, I have something to say to you. You know how much I love you and how happy you make me whenever I am with you and, as he got down on one knee, Kathryn Collier, I would like for you to be my wife. I want to take care of you and love you for all eternity." "Oh Jon I cried, are you serious?" "I've never been more serious," Jon responded. Say yes and make me the happiest man in the world. "Yes, yes," I shouted as we embraced and gave each other a long and sensual kiss. Jon took my hand and slid the most beautiful ring on my finger. "Oh Jon, that is the loveliest ring I have ever seen in my life, I can't wait to tell my folks." "They already know. I asked your Dad for your hand in marriage this morning before breakfast; he and your Mother gave us their blessing. I knew the perfect place to propose to you was by your peaceful river, and under this beautiful maple tree." "Yes Jon, you're right, this is the perfect place".

Our Christmas couldn't have been more wonderful. We had several days of visiting and walks by the river, then it was time to return to the City. I couldn't wait to tell Mrs. Barrett what a wonderful holiday we had, and to tell her of my and Jon's engagement. She will be thrilled, she just loves Jon.

Chapter 25

Preparations for The Wedding

Winter quickly turned to spring, and Jon and I were planning a June wedding. There was so much to be done. Jon was going to ask Curtis to be his best man and have Peter and Brady as groomsmen. I always planned to have Sarah, my high school friend, as my matron of honor. Sarah's five-year-old son, Randy as the ring bearer. Emily who had first trained me at the Law Firm would be my bridesmaid. Her daughter Ruby was to be the flower girl. Of course, Dad would give me away. I also wanted Mother to walk down the aisle with us. Jon's parents would also be involved. I wanted to make sure Mrs. Barrett held a seat of prominence as well. I had asked Jon's two sisters to light the candles.

I chose sage green with pink sashes for the girl's dresses, and sage green dresses for both Mothers. The girls would carry small bouquets of pink rose buds tied with pink and sage ribbon. The little flower girl would wear a miniature version of the other dresses. A halo of pink rose buds and white baby breath tied with pink and sage ribbons, set atop her golden curls. The men in the wedding party would all wear black tuxedos with white shirts and sage green vests and ties.

The wedding would be at the Missionary Alliance Church where Jon and I had been attending. The reception to be in the Church Hall. It was a beautiful room and easy to decorate for a summer wedding reception. Mother and I planned a date to go into the city to shop for my wedding gown. I had also asked Jon's Mother to come with us and have a special part in the gown selection. She was such a sweet and kind woman and I knew she and I would have a long and loving relationship in the years to come.

I had a mental picture of what I wanted my gown to look like but finding it would be another story. There were several bridal shops and I was hoping to find all the dresses at the same shop. Jon was taking care of the men's tuxedos and the ring bearer. He was also getting the 'thank you' gifts for the men in the wedding party. That would be a big help for me. However, we still had to squeeze in our continued work at the Law Firm. Curtis was taking a lot of Jon's work while we were planning the wedding. Everyone was excited and eager to help.

We had set the date to go dress shopping. Emily, her little girl Ruby, and Sarah would meet up with myself, my and Jon's Mom's for lunch. It was going to be a fun day.

Preparations for The Wedding

The shopping day finally rolled around, and I was extremely excited. We first met at a little outdoor restaurant, had a nice lunch then went to the Bridal shop. First, I wanted to look for the girl's dresses and both Mother's dresses. The clerk was very helpful showing us what they had. She also had a catalog of various designs and fabrics. I opened the book and there were the dresses for the girls! I couldn't believe my eyes. They were sleeveless with a scooped neckline and fitted to the waist. The flowing skirt was tufted to the floor. Around the waist was a large satin sash which flowed down the back of the dress. The picture showed it floor length, which was what I had planned and hoped to find. They also showed matching shoes which were perfect. We could order them in sage green with a soft pink sash and could get the same style for the little flower girl. I was thrilled.

They also had the same sage silky material in a dress with a jacket that would be perfect for Mother. It was a simple straight dress with a fitted jacket. They had it in stock and in Mother's size. I insisted she try it on. She looked beautiful!

For Jon's Mother, we selected a two-piece fitted suit in the same shade of sage green. It was a simple jacket with beautiful buttons down the front and an A-line skirt. It was perfect for her figure. She, like my Mother, was a small slender woman.

Now it was time to look for the wedding gown. I first scanned the catalog, but not seeing anything that caught my eye. The clerk suggested I look at some of the dresses they had on the rack. She went into the dress area which had hundreds of wedding gowns and emerged with two gowns in each hand lifted high over her head. One of the dresses mirrored the other dresses we had chosen for the attendants. It had clusters of pearls and sequins at the bottom of each big tuck. The fabric was a beautiful heavy white satin. The bodice was fitted with a scooped neckline and small cap sleeves with hundreds of pearls and sequins. It sparkled like my new diamond ring. The outer edge of the veil was trimmed in a beautiful lace and scattered with more pears and sequins. I went into the dressing room and the clerk slipped the dress down over my head. She began to pull the very long zipper in the back which was lined with many tiny cover buttons. The gown had to be gathered in the back with large clothes pins as this dress was four sizes too large. The store could order my size in the dress, if this was the gown I chose. When she turned me around to look in the mirror, it took my breath away. I was in love with this gown and veil and knew Jon would be pleased with it too. It was perfect.

When I walked out of the dressing room where Mother, Jon's Mother, Sarah and Emily were waiting, they all gasped with delight. "Oh, Kathryn, it's lovely," Mother said as a tear slowly slid down her cheek. "It is Sarah said, it couldn't be more perfect for you Kathryn." "They always say when the bride's Mother cries, that's the dress," the clerk exclaimed, as she handed Mother a tissue.

I couldn't believe we had found the perfect dresses in one afternoon. The clerk took careful measurements and said she would order the

Preparations for The Wedding

gowns the next day. When the gowns arrived, they would contact us for a fitting and if any additional alterations were required, there would be plenty of time to do them.

The wedding plans began to fall into place. Jon and I had taken one afternoon from the Law Firm to select the cake and flowers. I wanted him to be involved in the entire wedding selections. We had met with Pastor Chris several times. He had led us in a premarital class to teach us about God's instructions for a married couple. This teaching will make our life happier, and smooth out the rough spots that all newlyweds seem to encounter.

We had decided to send out invitations only to those out of town guests and have an open invitation to the whole Church. The wedding was scheduled for June 4th at 2:00 p.m., reception immediately following the wedding in the Church Hall. Cake and punch would be served. The florist was to move the large baskets of flowers from the Sanctuary to the Hall and placed them on each side of the serving table.

The plans seemed to be going great, everything was falling into place. Then, one afternoon I received a call from the bridal shop. My gown had been back ordered. I couldn't believe my ears. How could everything be going so smoothly and suddenly this major problem emerges. I hung up the phone and called Jon with a tearful voice and told him of the problem. "Well," he said, "can't you just get another dress?" How could he be so causal about the whole situation, get another dress? Did he really think it would be that easy?

THE RIVER OF LIFE

Was he out of his mind? My heart pounded; I felt sick to my stomach. I called the bridal shop back and told them I would be down tomorrow to see what suggestions they might have for getting my gown in time for our wedding.

The next afternoon, I rushed down to the bridal shop to see what could be done. In the meantime, the Bridal Shop had contacted their main suppliers. They were all checking to see if perhaps one Bridal Shop may have that gown in stock. If they had the gown in a larger size, it could easily be altered in plenty of time. They were trying very hard to get the gown for my wedding. They discussed their plan with me and ask to give them a couple of days. I went back home feeling a little better that possibly, there was a gown out there somewhere for me.

Three days went by and the Bridal Shop called. The clerk had sounded optimistic when I answered the phone. "Well," she said, "we have good news. We have found the gown. However, it's two sizes larger, so we will need to start your first fitting when the gown arrives into our shop." "That's not a problem," I told her. "I will come in the middle of the night if I need to." A soft giggle came from the other end of the phone. "I know how frustrating these problems are for new brides, however, we experience these situations almost weekly," the clerk explained. "I hope I was not too much of a pain for you to deal with." "Not at all," she said kindly, as I thanked her, and we hung up.

Four days later the bridal shop called, and my gown had arrived. I made an appointment to go

Preparations for The Wedding

for my fitting, so they could start the alterations. It looked like I would be walking down the aisle wearing this beautiful gown after all.

The shop had received the other dresses earlier and everyone had gone down for their fittings and now everyone's dress fit great. Yea, the wedding plans were back on track. Everything had been ordered. The flowers, cake, 'thank you gifts' all purchased and wrapped, the rehearsal dinner planned, and the invitations were all mailed with returned RSVP'S received. Jon had totally taken care of the tuxes and 'thank you' gifts for the men in the wedding party.

June 2nd rolled around, and my Mother and Dad came to the city and stayed with Mrs. Barrett and me. My brothers stayed with one of their friends and Jon's parents and sisters also arrived and were staying at Jon's apartment. We had the rehearsal dinner at a small Italian restaurant close to the Church on Friday night. After the rehearsal and dinner, my parents, Jon's family, and Jon and I went back to Mrs. Barrett's to visit for a while. I loved my new family, they were loving, just like mine. They had the same religious and moral values as my parents and brothers. Our families were a perfect match.

Saturday morning, I was up early. I had my morning devotion, praising God and thanking Him for my wonderful life that was beginning to unfold. I had tea & toast with Mrs. Barrett and Mother, while Dad slept in. I wanted to get an early start, as there seemed so much had to be done before the wedding on Sunday afternoon. I had called both the florist and the bakery to make sure everything was still on schedule for Sunday deliveries. Church service would be over at 12:00 noon. They had only two hours to bring in the flowers, set up the cake table, and the guest book table. However, they assured me they could handle it, and everything would be done on time before the guests began to arrive. I thanked each of them and hung up the phone.

I went out on the porch where Mother and Mrs. Barrett had moved to finish their tea. I began to chatter like a nervous bride. Mother laughed, "Kathryn Collier, I have never seen you so nervous, giddy and excited in my life." "I know Mother, there must be something I need to do." "I know I am forgetting something important." "How in the world could you have forgotten anything Kathryn," Mrs. Barrett said, "you have worked on this wedding for months and have kept extensive notes," as she finished with a giggle and a big smile. "I know Mrs. Barrett, but nothing ever goes perfectly, there can always be an unexpected event that can ruin the whole day." "It's those 'not so perfect' occasions that hold the best memories. So, if something doesn't go perfectly, remember that," Mrs. Barrett said. "I'll try," as I went back into the kitchen to get the teapot to refill all the cups. Just as I sat down the phone rang. "You better get it Kathryn, it's probably for you," Mrs. Barrett said. I ran into the living room and grabbed the phone with an anxious, 'hello'? "Kathryn? Is everything alright," Jon said nervously." "Oh hi Jon, yes everything is fine." "You know me, I'm always expecting the

Preparations for The Wedding

worse news and today of all days totally expect it." "You've got to quit that Kathryn, am I going to live with a 'nervous nelly' that can never relax and enjoy life?" "I hope not," I said with an embarrassed voice.

Jon told me he was going to look over a couple of cases in the office and turn them over to Curtis. Then, he planned to come by and visit with me, Mrs. Barrett and my folks. Later that evening Jon had made plans to take his parents and sisters, my parents and brothers, Mrs. Barrett and I out to this quaint little restaurant he and Curtis had accidently found. This would be nice. We can all relax and enjoy each other's company. This will be the last evening Jon and I spend with our parents and family before the wedding. We will be leaving for our honeymoon immediately following the reception. Jon had planned our honeymoon and I only knew we were going on a Caribbean Cruise. Beyond that, I was clueless. Jon loved to surprise me, that was his joy in life. And, I loved surprises, so it all worked.

Chapter 26

My and Jon's Wedding Day

I woke early on Sunday morning, said my morning prayer asking for a great day and thanking God for allowing me to marry such a wonderful man.

I hurriedly took my shower as I was meeting Sarah and Emily at the hairdresser to have our hair and makeup done promptly at 9:00 a.m. Then, back to Mrs. Barrett's, where she and Mother had planned a light lunch. Jon and I had promised each other, we would not see or even speak on the phone today. Unless, it was an emergency. We were saving everything for the first time we saw each other at the end of the aisle.

After finishing at the hairdresser, I returned to Mrs. Barrett's. She and Mother were just sitting the lunch on the table. I ate a little but was so nervous and excited, food just didn't want to go down. After lunch, I finished my packing for the honeymoon and picked up a book to relax before getting dressed. Mother, Dad and Mrs. Barrett were already getting ready when Mother noticed I was sitting reading. "Kathryn, are you going to the wedding with us?" She said smiling. "I know Mother, I was just trying to relax a bit before dressing." "I think I am ready to pull it together now though." As Mother came into my room and closed the door behind her, she had a different look on her face. She sat down on the bed beside me, took my hands and looked at me with teary eyes. "Kathryn, your Dad and I are so proud of you. You are a wonderful daughter and I know will make Jon a fabulous wife and eventually be an excellent Mother. I just want you to know how much we love you and how excited we are for you, as you enter the next phase of your life." She took me in her arms and held me tight for a few seconds as we both began to sob softly. "You're the greatest parents too Mother, the boys and I are so fortunate to have been raised by Christian parents and living in the greatest place in the world, just steps from that wonderful river."

Mother reached for the tissue box and pulled a tissue for both of us, as we began to laugh. "I hope this is the last of the tears for today," Mother. "Me too dear, but I'm not making any promises." Now, let's get you into that beautiful gown so you can marry that handsome man. Mother carefully took the gown off the hanger, gathered up the skirt and lifted it high above my head as I guided my arms into it. It smelled of new satin fabric, sweet and clean, a smell I will remember for the rest of my life. Mother pulled the skirt down and began to pull up the long zipper. I sat down at the mirror as Mother took my veil and carefully placed it above the curls

My and Jon's Wedding Day

on the back of my dark hair. "Oh Kathryn," she said as I stood and turned toward her, "you look amazing." "Is it ok if I asked your Dad to come in and see you?" "Absolutely, I want him to see his little girl all grown up," I responded as I snickered. Mother left the room and shortly, Dad appeared at the door. He came in and closed the door behind him and just stood for what seemed like several seconds before he finally said, "Kathryn, I have never seen a more beautiful bride in all my life." I just want to tell you how much I love you and to always remember, put the Lord first in your lives and everything will work out. Your Mother and I have tried it and believe me, it really works. I know Dad, I'm thankful you have always trusted God, and no matter what, we will too.

Mother helped me gather my gown up carefully as I crawled into the back seat of the car. Dad was driving me to the Church and Mrs. Barrett and Mother were coming in Mrs. Barrett's car. We arrived at the back entrance of the Church the same time Emily, Sarah and their children arrived. We all hugged, then went into the bridal room of the Church to wait for 2:00 p.m. Sarah went to peek at the decorated sanctuary. She came back with a truly beautiful report. "The Church looks amazing Kathryn, you are going to be so pleased." There are four huge ferns behind the large four candelabras with tall white tapers and large white satin bows on the front of each candelabrum. Then, at the bottom of the steps leading to the stage area are two baskets of beautiful white star gazer lilies, white roses, white hydrangeas, babies' breath

THE RIVER OF LIFE

and several other white flowers. There is a white runner extending the entire length of the aisle. "It sounds beautiful Sarah; I can't wait to see it."

Suddenly, soft music began to play, and we could hear footsteps and light voices as the guests began to arrive and be seated. My body became tense, my mouth was dry, and I felt like I was going to cry. What is this I thought, I'm about to have the most beautiful experience of my entire life and all at once my body seemed to be deceiving me. I took a drink of water and began to try to relax. It worked.

Sarah peeked through a tiny crack in the door and announced that Jon, the pastor and my brothers were at the front of the Church. Jon's parents were being seated and Jon's sisters were lighting the candles.

At once, the music began to play which signaled Sarah and Emily to start down the aisle. They both hugged me and slowly took their turn down the aisle. Then following them was Sarah's little boy Randy, and Emily's little girl Ruby. Emily was concerned that little Ruby may back out at the last minute, but it looked like she was going to make it after all. She slowly and meticulously took each rose petal from her basket and carefully dropped it to the floor. Sarah's little boy, Randy was carrying the ring pillow as if it were precious cargo, very carefully and not taking his eyes off it. It was so precious, and I knew Emily and Sarah were both happy mothers seeing their children coming down the aisle.

My and Jon's Wedding Day

My Mother and Dad both took turns, as we kissed and hugged each other. Then double doors opened wide and at the end of the aisle, I could see Jon. He looked incredibly handsome and had the biggest smile on his face I have ever seen. As the music changed to 'Here comes the Bride' everyone rose to their feet as my parents and I started the walk down the aisle.

Suddenly, I could think of nothing except how much I loved that tall, handsome man. Finally, we reached the stage and Mother turned to me and kissed my cheek and whispered, "I love you my darling." Then, Pastor Chris began to speak. "Who gives this woman to be married to this man?" "Her Mother and I" my Dad said in a soft nervous voice. My Dad turned to me and squeezed me tightly as he whispered, "Kathryn, you look so beautiful." "Thank you, Dad," I whispered, "I love you so much." Then Jon stepped forward as Dad took my hand and put it in Jon's. Dad hugged Jon before taking his seat next to Mother.

The ceremony was beautiful. After Pastor Chris read some scriptures and explained the Lord's instructions for a husband and wife's successful marriage, it was time to light the Unity candle. Mother and Jon's mother both came up onto the stage, each took a long white lighted candle, and walked to the center toward the table where the Unity candle sat. They both in unison lit the candle, blew out their candles, embraced and took their seats.

Jon and I had requested we take Communion. After it was served to us the ceremony continued.

THE RIVER OF LIFE

Pastor Chris read the vows and Jon and I read what we had both written for this next part of the ceremony. Now it was time for the giving and receiving of rings. All went well with my ring. However, when I started to put Jon's ring on his finger, my hands were trembling so much I almost dropped the ring, then Jon's hand was extremely sweaty, and the ring was refusing to go on his finger. As I continued to push the ring, Jon and I both began to laugh quietly. This was the moment Mrs. Barrett was referring to, a moment not so perfect, but one we would remember for the rest of our lives. Finally, the ring went on and Jon and I both gave a soft sigh of relief. Pastor Chris continued after making a funny remark about the ring problem. The congregation softly chuckled. Now I felt more relaxed and really enjoyed the rest of the ceremony.

Finally, it was time for Pastor Chris to announce we were husband and wife and that Jon could kiss his bride. This was the moment I had been waiting for. Jon held me tight and gave me a soft but loving kiss, then another little peck on my cheek as Pastor Chris asked the congregation to stand and he introduced us as Mr. and Mrs. Jon Davis. Everyone applauded as the music began to play and Jon and I, arm in arm, walked down the aisle to the back of the Church.

Jon kissed me again quickly and told me how much he loved me and how happy he was. The rest of the bridal party made their way toward the back of the Church. The Pastor had announced there would be a reception in the Church Hall immediately following the ceremony, so the guests slowly

My and Jon's Wedding Day

moved toward the Hall, stopping to congratulate us. The bridal party remained in the Sanctuary for pictures and after what seemed a lot of pictures; we finally entered the Hall with much applause and greetings from our guests.

Jon and I mingled among the guests and soon it was time to cut the cake. The reception table was covered with a beautiful hand-made linen cloth Mrs. Barrett purchased when she had been in London. The cake was beautiful all in white with a lot of scroll work, roses and other flowers, and on top was a gorgeous arrangement of fresh flowers mirroring the large baskets of white flowers which sit at each end of the reception table.

The ladies of the Church had put out the Church's white dessert plates, crystal glasses and silver forks. The punch was in a beautiful crystal bowl with a lovely glass ladle which was given to me by my favorite Aunt Virginia Lou before she passed away years earlier. Mother had told her sister, she would save the crystal bowl and ladle for me to be used at my wedding. I felt my precious Aunt was looking down from heaven today and was happy to see what a beautiful wedding I had and the wonderful man I would be sharing my life with.

Jon and I stood behind the cake as we both held the silver knife to cut the cake. Jon looked at me and whispered, "no cake in the face huh?" "No Jon please, we made a deal, remember?" "I'm just teasing," as he put his arm around me and gave a little squeeze. "I wouldn't do anything to mess up how beautiful you look at this moment." We cut the cake and gave each other a small bite, then it was time for a toast with the punch. We had received two beautiful champagne glasses with our initials engraved on them as one of our wedding gifts. Our glasses were filled with punch and ready. We wrapped our hands around each other's as Jon's Dad gave a beautiful toast.

After everyone was served, cake and punch consumed, it was time to leave. Everyone followed us out of the Hall as I prepared to toss my bouquet. As luck would have it, one of Jon's sisters caught the bouquet. She was thrilled; however, Jon's Mother looked a bit perplexed as she was insistent both girls should finish college before marriage. "It's only a tradition Mother," Jon's sister laughingly told her. "I know, I just want to make sure you know it," she said with emphasis as they both laughed and hugged each other.

Peter pulled Jon's car around front which he and Brady had so lavishly decorated with shave crème, crape paper, cans tied to the back and written 'Just Married' on the back window. Jon helped me into the car as we waved our arms out the window and drove away.

Chapter 27

Honeymoon

We went to Mrs. Barrett's house, changed our clothes and waited for Curtis to take us to the airport. Jon's parents were going to load the gifts into their car and take them to Jon's apartment. We would get everyone together for 'gift opening' when we returned from our honeymoon.

After our plane landed, we took a cab to the Cruise Ship and soon it was time to board. I was so excited, I had never been on a Cruise, but had always heard of the wonderful food and all the things available to do. We were shown to our cabin by a nice young man. He said he would be taking care of all our needs while we were on the Cruise and if we needed anything, just let him know. After he put our bags in our cabin, he left.

Suddenly, I was alone with my husband, and for the first time, I felt like a married woman. Jon and I both started to unpack our bags and put our things in the drawers and closet. I didn't realize how small they can make a room with a bed and a little storage, but small it was. After Jon and I

THE RIVER OF LIFE

unpacked, we decided to go up on deck to watch the ship pull away from the dock. There were tons of people waving to their loved ones on the dock and were shouting to those on board to have a good time. We waved back although we didn't know anyone. After the ship had pulled away, Jon and I went to the dining hall and had a wonderful meal. We walked around the deck for a bit, then decided to go to our cabin.

Sarah and Emily had given me a lovely white satin gown and robe to wear on my wedding night. The bodice of the gown was scattered with tiny pearls and had spaghetti straps. The robe also had pearls with short cap sleeves, both were floor length. It was the most beautiful set of sleepwear I had ever seen. I went into the bathroom and began to remove my clothes to take a shower. Just as I was about to remove my underwear, Jon opened the door and I let out a loud scream. "Oh my gosh Kathryn, I am so sorry." Jon said. "I should have knocked; I was just going to brush my teeth." That's ok Jon; I will be out as soon as I finish my shower. I was so embarrassed to think I screamed at Jon as if he was a stranger breaking into my room. This marriage thing will take some getting used to, but I'm sure we can work it out, I thought to myself.

The five days on the ship flew by quickly and it was time for us to get off and back to the airport. Jon had not told me what the remainder of our honeymoon was going to include. I didn't know when or where we were headed. When our flight landed, and had our luggage, we saw Curtis waving and

Honeymoon

yelling at us as we came down the escalator. We were glad to see him. It was nice of him to be there to pick us up. I noticed Jon whisper something to Curtis and he shook his head 'yes' and Jon seemed pleased. I had no idea what they had up their sleeves but was eager to go along with whatever.

Curtis took us to Jon's apartment, which was now my new home. My parents and Mrs. Barrett had moved my belongings while we were gone. It would be strange not living with Mrs. Barrett any longer, I had stayed with her for seven years, although when I first moved in, I assumed it would be for only a few weeks. I loved being with Mrs. Barrett and was going to miss her terribly but would be able to visit her often. She made me promise I would come for lunch at least once a week.

Chapter 28

The Wedding Surprise

After Jon carried me over the threshold and brought in the luggage, he grabbed the car keys and said, "well, Mrs. Davis, would you like to find out what the other surprise is? Of course, I can't wait to see what you have been so secretive about. As we got into the car, Jon pulled out a blindfold and said, well Mrs. Davis, I'm going to have to ask you to put this on for the remainder of the trip. Jon started the car and began to drive. I couldn't tell which direction we were going, if we were headed into the City or out toward the country. We drove for about twenty minutes and Jon began to slow the car. We're almost there, Mrs. Davis. Suddenly, the car came to a stop and I could hear Jon getting out and closed his door. He opened my door and helped me from the car. Now Kathryn, you can remove your blindfold. Happy wedding gift, this is the rest of the honeymoon surprise. Words failed me as I grabbed Jon around the neck and swung my legs around his waist. Jon, you are an

THE RIVER OF LIFE

amazing husband, I can't tell you how happy and excited I am at this moment.

In front of me was this beautiful house I had been talking about for months. It had just been completed when I had told Jon I saw a 'for sale' sign down by the entrance to the new house. I just wonder who will buy it I had thought at the time; I would love to live out here in the country in this house someday. However, I never thought for one moment Jon would be the one to buy it. It was a white two story with four dormer windows on the second floor. It had a beautiful dark green roof and a porch that went around the entire front and side of the house. It had a three-car garage and a cute little gazebo in the side yard. The yard was beautifully landscaped with lots of shrubs and beautiful plants. There was a huge oak tree at the corner of the yard which appeared as if the house was built around it just to complete the grandeur of that tree. There was a white rail fence around the property and at the entrance to the drive was a beautiful iron decorative gate with stone post on both sides.

Can we get in to see the house, I excitedly asked Jon. Yes, that is what Curtis and I was talking about at the airport. I was asking him if he had the gate controls and the key to the house. This is your house Kathryn, I hope we spend many happy years in this house. I want us to raise lots of kids and even have grandchildren coming to spend weekends and holidays with us. Easy, Jon, let's don't get ahead of ourselves; I said laughing at Jon's already having not only children, but grandchildren. But that was my hope as well.

The Wedding Surprise

As Jon opened the front door, I could tell immediately, this was truly my dream home. In the foyer was a grand curved stairway with white spindles and oak railing. The steps were a beautiful lustrous oak. It had a vaulted ceiling with a very large light hanging from the ceiling. When you turned to the left was a huge vaulted ceiling living room with windows on two sides that went from floor to ceiling. In the middle of the ceiling was a beautiful hanging light. On the wall between large white book shelves was a gorgeous white marble fireplace. The walls were painted a soft taupe with white crown moldings and tall baseboards. A large arched doorway led into the dining room. It too had one wall of floor to ceiling windows and on another wall was a beautiful built-in china cabinet with glass doors. My wedding china would look lovely behind those glass doors. Leaving the dining area you entered the kitchen. The kitchen walls were covered with a creamy white bead board, dark cherry cupboards and beautiful white Formica countertops. The appliances were all white porcelain. And off to one side of the kitchen was a walk-in pantry. On the other side of the kitchen was a rounded breakfast nook, which again had the long windows and a lovely light fixture. A round table for this area will be perfect, I told Jon as my decorating wheels were spinning. Adjoining the kitchen was a large family room and on the back of the house was a totally glassed sunroom which looked out onto the garden. There was a master suite on the other side of the house with a spacious master bath. Beyond the master suite was

THE RIVER OF LIFE

a large office with dark cherry built in bookshelves and the entire room was covered with dark cherry paneling. Beautiful sconces graced the walls every few feet. The coffered ceiling was also done in cherry wood. Hanging in the center of the room was a very large light which took on a masculine appearance. I could picture a very large cherry desk in this room which would be perfect for Jon's home office.

Upstairs were three more bedrooms and another master suite. There were also three more bathrooms and a small sitting area.

There was a large unfinished basement, but Jon wanted to finish it himself after we had a family and knew what our needs are. From a small hall off the kitchen was a mudroom and a door. I ask Jon where this door lead and he said oh, that's just the garage, but you can look in it if you want to. Jon seemed to wonder off into another room just as I opened the door. There, in the garage was a beautiful white convertible. Jon, I shrieked, there's a new car in our garage! Really, he gasped. I wonder who that belongs to. I walked into the garage, opened the car door and on the steering wheel was a card with my name on it. It read: Kathryn, congratulations, you have just won a new car. This is your final surprise. I love you with all my heart, Jon.

Jon, I screamed, as I jumped into his arms. This all seems like a wonderful dream. I'm afraid I'm going to wake up. You're not dreaming sweetheart, this is reality and we have a new house and

The Wedding Surprise

you have a new car. Are you happy? Happy isn't the word for it, I'm overwhelmed with joy.

Now, Mrs. Davis, you have a lot of decorating and furniture shopping to do. I don't think I have any furniture in my apartment that will be fit for your new house. We'll see, I told him, don't throw anything out just yet. Ok, whatever you say Mrs. Davis, as he locked the door and we walked to the car.

Chapter 29

My Dad's Heart Attack

In the weeks to follow, John and I moved the things from his apartment to the new house. We kept most of the furniture, this will work for now. I wanted to take my time furnishing and decorating the house. Sometimes, as you live in a house for a few months you have different ideas. I was leaning toward French Country style and had kept a book of different pictures from magazines. I had also purchased several decorating books to help me. I knew I loved yellows, reds, greens and a lot of floral fabrics. Jon kept encouraging me to get whatever I wanted for the house, but until I was certain, I was waiting.

The remainder of the summer went by quickly and we were both working long hours at the office. When I had an extra minute, I was still thinking about the house, and how I would eventually decorate it.

I had received a letter from Mother saying Dad was not feeling well and they had an appointment to go see the Dr. I was concerned as I had noticed

THE RIVER OF LIFE

the last time we had visited, Dad seemed tired and looked pale. If there was anything serious, Mother would call me.

My Dad was never ill. When we were kids, he was the only one who never got a cold or the flu. When the rest of the family would be bed ridden, he would be waiting on us. But now, I had a sick feeling in my stomach about Dad. I tried to push my thoughts to the back of my mind as I continued to go over the files at the office.

One fall evening, while Jon and I sat in the gazebo enjoying the early fall sounds and the dark star filled night, the phone in the house rang. Jon jumped and ran toward the back porch yelling over his shoulder, "it's probably Curtis calling about one of our court cases for tomorrow." After a very short moment, Jon came to the back and called out to me, Kathryn, you better come in and take this call, it's your Mother. I ran as quickly as my feet would carry me and grabbed the phone from Jon's hand.

"Mother! Mother! what is it? I screamed." I could hear her sobbing uncontrollably on the other end of the phone. Once again, I yelled, "Mother, what is wrong?" "Kathryn, you need to come home. It's your Father, he's had a massive heart attack. He is in the hospital and well, they don't think he will make it." "Oh dear God, no, no!" I cried as I slowly dropped to my knees.

Jon quickly wrapped his strong arms around my shoulders and lifted me gently to the chair. He took the phone from my hand and began speaking with Mother, as I continued to sob. I could hear

My Dad's Heart Attack

him saying yes, yes, we will Mom. Jon hung up the phone.

Jon lifted me from the chair and held me tight while stroking my hair, trying desperately to console me. Oh Jon, I can't survive without my Dad, life will stop for me as well as for my Mother. What in the world will she do if anything happens to Dad? Kathryn, Jon said, as he lifted my tear-filled face in his strong hands. What is the first thing we have been taught to do when problems and heartache comes our way? We give it to God and ask Him to take care of your Dad. Remember, He is the great physician and we must trust Him and lean on Him in these trying times. He knows your heart and how much you love your Dad. Let's give this to our Heavenly Father. At that moment Jon and I both dropped to our knees and began to pray.

We threw a few things together, and soon were on our way. We arrived at the hospital in record time. Jon let me out at the Emergency Room entrance, while he parked the car. I ran through three sets of glass doors and finally arrived at the Emergency waiting room desk.

I'm looking for my Mother, Ethel Collier. She is with my Dad, Chris Collier who has had a heart attack. The woman lifted a long clip board and ran her finger down the list. Oh yes, here he is. They have moved Mr. Collier to the Cardiac wing. Take the elevator up to the third floor and follow the signs to the cardiac information desk. They can give you his room number. Thank you, I said trembling as I ran back toward the glass doors waiting for Jon. When he arrived, we followed the

THE RIVER OF LIFE

instructions and raced to the third floor Cardiac Wing. Breathless, I ran to the desk. I asked the nurse if she could please tell me what room Mr. Chris Collier is in? She turned around to another desk and looked at a long chart. She turned back and said, he is in room 352.

Jon and I quickly walked down the hall to Dad's room. The door was closed so I lightly knocked. Mother opened the door and the look on her face told me the news was not good. She grabbed me and pulled me back into the hall. Mother, what have they told you about Dad's condition? Well, I was able to speak with his doctor about an hour ago and he said for the time being, your Dad is stable. We will have to wait a couple of days for more tests so they can determine how much damage the heart attack did. If the news is good, he can be kept stable with medications until he is able to undergo bypass surgery. The Doctor said if he remains stable for the next 24 hours, his chances of survival are pretty good.

"Oh Mother," I said as I grabbed her and held her tight. "I am so thankful, I was afraid Dad would be gone before Jon and I got here. I wanted to be able to tell Dad how much I love him." Have you been able to reach Peter and Brady yet? Yes, I have talked with both boys. Peter will be here tonight, and Brady will come tomorrow, after he is finished with one of his final exams.

Oh Kathryn, I am so glad you are here with me. I can't imagine life without your Dad. I know Mother, I have had the same fear. Jon and I will stay with you until we are sure Dad remains stable.

My Dad's Heart Attack

Jon will have to return to the Firm in the next couple of days, but I will stay on. Thanks Kathryn that will be a big help for me, Mother said as she squeezed my hand.

As the next few days passed, Dad began to look much better and remained stable as the Doctors continued to run more test. For now, the prognosis for Dad's recovery looked good. He would however, in the future need to undergo bypass surgery. The next few months would tell the Doctors when Dad's surgery would be scheduled.

Dad was released from the hospital and continued to improve. I was staying at home with the folks, while Jon was working many hours at the Firm. When I was sure Dad was on the road to recovery, I told my parents, I needed to return to the City and get back to work. Of course, they understood my urgency to be back at the Firm. Jon and Curtis had many cases that needed a lot of research.

Chapter 30

Unexpected Surprise for Jon

The weeks and months swiftly flew by as Jon and I worked many hours at the Firm. The Law practice was growing at a rapid pace and we thought of nothing but work. It seemed we would go to work, be there for many hours, come home, eat, shower and drop into bed. The long hours seemed to be affecting my health.

As fall and winter approached, I picked up a flu bug that I couldn't seem to shake. I had stayed home the first couple of days due to constant vomiting and dizziness that pretty much kept me on the couch. It seemed I was the only one in the office who had this flu bug. I had no idea where I picked up the germ. I just knew it had a good hold on me. Finally, after a couple of weeks of feeling so crummy, Jon insisted I see the Doctor. I reluctantly made the appointed for Tuesday afternoon at 2:00 p.m.

THE RIVER OF LIFE

The girl at the front desk called my name for my appointment. I followed a young nurse into the examination room. She weighed me, checked my temperature, blood pressure, and laid my file on the desk. She told me the Dr. would be in shortly.

Dr. Blackman came into the room and greeted me. He asked me about my condition and how I was feeling. I told him I was always so dizzy and seemed to vomit for no reason. He looked in my nose, ears, and mouth and seemed puzzled. Well Kathryn, I can't explain the dizziness as you don't seem to have an ear infection. It does look like you have lost a little weight since you were in last. How often and when do you vomit? Well, almost the minute my feet hit the floor. I am so nauseous, I run to the bathroom and am so sick, I told him.

Well, let's get a urine sample and see if we can figure this out, as he nodded toward the nurse. She came back into the room, handed me a plastic cup, and sent me into the restroom to get the sample. She took the sample and told me to wait in the examination room while the Doctor saw another patient. The Dr. would be back in to see me after the lab was finished with the sample.

I picked up a magazine and flipped through the pages for about 15 minutes when Doctor Blackman finally returned. Well Kathryn, I think we have this little problem figured out. "Thank goodness, I said with relief. When will I start to feel better?" "Well I think in about 7½ months, you will be your old self again." It took me by surprise. I sat there with my mouth open. "You're expecting a child Kathryn. It looks like you are about 6 weeks pregnant." What?

Unexpected Surprise for Jon

I couldn't believe my ears. How could I have missed the signs? I knew my cycle had been a little off, but I blamed my long exhausting hours at the office and then when I got the 'flu bug', I again blamed that on my late cycle.

This will be a huge shock to Jon, but I knew he would be thrilled. It would take me a little while to take all this news in. Now, I had to figure out how to break the news to Jon. I wanted it to be special as Jon and I had been talking about starting a family. However, the office had kept us so busy, we had not even spoke of it recently. Now, without warning, this little person was marching into our lives.

As I got into my car to start home, I prayed God would protect our little one and give us a healthy baby. I thanked Him for this blessing, as I started the car and left the parking lot.

I stopped at the market and picked up two nice steaks, salad fixings, some wonderful bread, and a special bottle of wine. Although, I knew I would not drink the wine, Jon would enjoy it with steak, plus we needed something to toast with. I picked up a bouquet of flowers for the table. I planned to fix baked potatoes, make the salad and prepare the bread. I would light the grill when I knew Jon was on his way home. Jon always called me before he left the office, in case I needed him to pick up something from the market, or more Pepto-Bismol from the Drug Store.

When Jon called, I told him I had stopped at the market and they had some nice steaks, so I had gotten a couple and would light the grill waiting for

THE RIVER OF LIFE

him to come home and cook them. Great, he said, I'm starving.

How was your Doctor appointment? Are you going to live, he jokingly laughed softly? Well, I think so, but we will talk about it when you get home. For now, I am concerned about my steaks, so Jon Davis, move your bootie. Yes mam, right away mam, I'm on my way. Jon was such a jokester, I so loved him for his lighthearted personality. When I heard Jon pull into the garage, I had the steaks on a platter and the grill was hot. "Hurry and take that suit off, I shouted from the kitchen, the potatoes and bread are almost finished." I'm all over it dear, can't wait for a good dinner.

The doctor appointment was not mentioned until we were half way through the meal. Jon mentioned the bouquet of flowers on the table and noticed I had used the good plates.

Well, I hope all this fancy stuff means you will finally get over this flu bug and quit puking every morning and night. I hesitated, as I slowly took a bite of my potato and waved my fork in circular motion. Yes, Dr. Blackman said I would be fine in about 7½ months. Really, Jon looked frightened, you mean it's going to take that long to get rid of a flu bug? Then immediately, Jon was struck with reality. Kat, Kat, are you telling me we're going to have a baby? Yes Daddy, that is exactly what I am telling you. Jon jumped from the table, overturning his chair, as he pulled me from the table and swung me around, while all the time laughing and yelling. Oh darling, you have made me the happiest man in the world. A baby, I can't believe

Unexpected Surprise for Jon

It. I know, I was caught off guard this afternoon when Dr. Blackman told me. He had pretty much ruled out everything when he asked me to give the nurse a urine sample, and even then, it didn't occur to me I could possibly be pregnant. Jon was still yelling. I can't wait to tell ole Curtis how lucky I am to become a father. I know, I'm so anxious to tell my folks too. Do you think we should wait until we are about 12 weeks in case the unthinkable could happen? Maybe you're right Kat, you're always the level headed one in the family. We must have a toast, I'll get you some water in a wine glass, Jon said as he rushed to the glass cabinet.

The next couple of weeks went by with my feeling very nauseous and dizzy. We had decided to wait to share our news with family and friends until we were approximately 12 weeks.

My next Doctor appointment would be when I was 9 weeks and Jon couldn't wait to go with me. When our appointment finally came Jon was excited to hear what the Dr. had to say. Dr. Blackman spoke with us at length and assured us everything looks good. I should just be patient for the sickness to go away, and then I could enjoy preparing for our little one. Jon and I continued to work at the Firm with me still not feeling the best. The minute I would get home from the office, I dropped on the couch and stayed there until bedtime. Jon would prepare us something to eat, then after a quick shower, I would go to bed. I was so hoping this dizzy, nauseous feeling would soon end.

THE RIVER OF LIFE

For the next two weeks, things seemed to improve slightly. I was not as dizzy as I had been, but still very nauseous.

On Monday afternoon, I felt so bad. I walked into Jon's office and without saying a word, he looked at me and said, Kat, go home, you look exhausted. I think I will Jon, as I picked up my jacket and handbag, said goodbye to the girls in the front office and headed for home.

I had only gone a couple of miles when I had the most excruciating pain in my stomach. The pain was unbearable as I struggled to make my way home. Finally, I pulled into the garage, slowly got out of the car and managed to open the door and walk to the living room and drop on the couch. I was in so much pain, I couldn't make it to the phone. I laid there for some time, then finally was able to crawl to the phone to call Jon. When he answered, I could barely speak. Jon, something is terribly wrong, please come home, I need to go to the Doctor.

I knew Jon would be scared and would drive like a crazy person getting home, but my pain was so intense, I didn't think to remind him to be careful. It seemed like only minutes when I heard his car in the garage and the door open quickly.

Kathryn, what's wrong? he said in a very nervous and scared voice. I don't know Jon, the pain hit me on the way home. I need to go to the bathroom but was afraid I couldn't make it by myself. Jon picked me up from the couch and carried me to the bathroom. I sat on the commode and suddenly,

Unexpected Surprise for Jon

I felt a gush of warm thick liquid. Oh Jon, I think my water just broke, as I cried uncontrollably.

I managed to pull myself together while Jon called the Doctor and told him I thought my water had broken. When we arrived at the hospital, the nurse assisted us into the patient room and said the Doctor would be right in. When Doctor Blackman opened the door, he had a concerned look on his face. Well, Kathryn and Jon, sometimes when a pregnancy is terminated, it only means it was not perfect. Let's give this a few hours and see if the pain continues. It's possible you have only lost some of the amniotic fluid and the baby will still be ok.

However, the pain only intensified as I lay on the table in the patient examination room. When the Doctor returned, he told us I would need a DNC. Jon looked at me with a trying to be strong look, but I knew we were both thinking why? Could we get pregnant again, or would we go through life without children? The surgery didn't take long. I stayed in the hospital overnight and Jon came back early Tuesday morning to pick me up. I was very weak, but most of all, I was disappointed. I felt guilty I had let Jon down; he was so thrilled to becoming a father.

I stayed home for a week and tried to get my strength back to return to work. Since we had not told anyone of my pregnancy, everyone thought I just had a bad flu bug, but was much better since I had spent a night in the hospital.

The next few months Jon and I kept busy with decorating the house and buying one or two pieces

THE RIVER OF LIFE

of furniture. I still didn't want to rush and was only doing one room at a time.

Chapter 31

Mrs. Barrett's Death

Mrs. Barrett had gone to spend time with her sister and niece. She told me during our phone call, she had not been feeling up to par recently. I had brushed it off as only the aging process for Mrs. Barrett and had not thought anymore about it.

Late one afternoon as we were getting ready to close the Firm and go home, Mrs. Barrett's niece called. She wanted to let us know Mrs. Barrett's Cancer had returned. Mrs. Barrett had not wanted her to tell us, she didn't want us to worry. Jon and I were devastated at the news. "I must go to her," I told Jon. Could he and Curtis handle things at the Firm for me to be gone a few days? Absolutely, Jon told me, I want you to be with Mrs. Barrett. I know she will be glad to have you with her.

My trip to my beloved Mrs. Barrett's seemed to take forever. I dreaded seeing her in pain and the sadness I would feel for her. She had supported me in my early days when I first arrived in the City and was such a loving and giving person.

THE RIVER OF LIFE

I prayed all the way to her sisters' house. When I arrived, her niece met me at the door with a look I was dreading to see. "The news is not good Kathryn," she said. She has gone down quickly in the last couple of days. I slowly opened the door to Mrs. Barrett's bedroom, she looked like she was sleeping. I quietly tiptoed to her bedside and took her hand.

She slowly opened her eyes and looked at me with a slight smile. "Oh Kathryn my darling," you didn't need to come and leave Jon to work at the Firm. I'm going to be fine. I know Mrs. Barrett, but I just wanted to pay you a little visit. I am so glad you did Kathryn, she said with a little broader smile. I plan to stay on for a few days, I know you don't really need me, but I have wanted to visit for some time. Oh, thank you Kathryn, it will be lovely to have you with me.

Mrs. Barrett, would you like me to make us a pot of tea? Oh, that would be lovely Kathryn, this will bring back old memories of having tea together. Ok, I will make our favorite raspberry tea, as I left Mrs. Barrett's bedroom and headed for the Kitchen.

My visit with Mrs. Barrett was a week and half. She continued to fight, but the cancer was stronger than she. Mrs. Barrett passed away in her sleep while I sat by her bedside reading to her. I called to tell Jon, and of course, when he heard my voice, he knew she was gone. Jon packed us some clothes and came to Mrs. Barrett's sisters for the funeral. My parents came too, as they loved her as much as Jon and me.

Mrs. Barrett's Death

I will never forget the loving way Mrs. Barrett took me into her home and gave me a lovely place to live when I was so young and trying to start a career. There will always be an empty place in my heart for Mrs. Barrett, but there will also be such loving memories I will hold onto forever.

Jon and I went back to Mrs. Barrett's home and helped her sister and niece clean out the house and put it on the market. The sight of seeing strangers coming into her home and taking her beloved possessions was hard for me. Mrs. Barrett's sister told me to take anything I wanted from the home. The one thing I would cherish was the lovely floral teapot Mrs. Barrett always used to make our delicious Raspberry tea. I know my sister would want you to have that teapot, she always spoke so fondly of you Kathryn. You brought so much joy into her life when you came to live with her. The feeling was mutual, I loved Mrs. Barrett so much and she brought so much happiness and joy into my life as well, I said to her sister.

Soon it was time for Jon and me to return home and get back to work at the Law Firm. Curtis had been able to hold down the fort but was truly glad when we were back working again. For the next few months, our routine became structured and simple, just go to work, back home, fix dinner, bedtime and repeat the process the next day. We had not talked much recently about trying to start our family again, but I knew it was on Jon's mind. We were not getting any younger and we wanted two children.

Chapter 32

Folks Aging

Spring and summer soon gave way to fall and the beautiful colors. We had made plans to visit my folks within the next couple of weeks while the trees along the riverbank would still be in the wonderful hue of color Jon and I both loved so much.

We arrived at my parent's home on Saturday morning. I was shocked at the way they both seemed to have aged in such a short span of time. My Dad especially seemed to have a grayish look in his face, and I had noticed when he would start to get up from his chair, he seemed to struggle. This was very hard for me to see my Dad like this. After all, he was only in his early 60's, and had always been such a strong robust man.

Mother was in the kitchen preparing a light lunch and I casually asked her how they both had been feeling. I didn't want her to know I had noticed they both looked tired and older. Well Kathryn, your Dad has not been feeling like himself lately, he seems to sit and just stare into space so much of the time. I'm not sure if he feels bad or

THE RIVER OF LIFE

if he's just thinking. I had wanted him to go back to his heart Dr. recently for a checkup, but he assures me he is ok and doesn't need to be seen by the Dr. again.

Mother then changed the subject by saying, don't you want to take your usual walk down by the river today dear? Yes, I told her. Jon and I will go after lunch and allow you and Dad to sit and rest. She agreed with my plan as she continued to sit the luncheon plates on the table.

After lunch, Jon and I quietly strolled down by the river. The trees were in such beautiful color it simply was breathtaking. Since Jon and I have been married, he has grown to love my river as much as I do. He always looks forward to coming home and seeing the different stages of beauty that surrounds my river. Jon mentioned what I had already realized that both my parents seemed to look more tired this trip than usual. I know, I'm really worried about them both but especially my Dad. I think my Mother is concerned too, and more than she lets on, I told Jon.

Jon and I stayed over the weekend, then returned home on Sunday evening. I couldn't help but continue to be alarmed about my parents, I would keep a close watch on them in the following weeks, then would return to spend Christmas with them. I was hoping they both seemed better by then.

Chapter 33

Everyone Home for Christmas

Christmas holiday arrived sooner than I was ready for it. Jon and I had done some quick shopping in the City one evening after we closed the Law Firm. I had bought gifts for my parents and two brothers, who would both be home for Christmas Holiday. My older brother Peter had announced to my parents, he would be bringing his new friend home with him for the family to meet. We were all excited about this, her name was Krista. Mother had called to tell me about Peter's plan to bring Krista. I was glad she had told me as I wanted to pick up a gift for her as well. I found a lovely scarf not knowing Krista, but I felt that it would go with most any coat or jacket and be warm for the cold winter days.

Peter had finally finished his Internship with a local Dentist and was ready to move out on his own. He had located a great building for his Dental practice in the City which was in the heart of a

THE RIVER OF LIFE

well-traveled area, next to a very popular mall. He had been busy hiring his staff and getting his Dental office open before the Holiday. We were all excited to hear all about his new life, especially, all about Krista.

Soon Jon and I had wrapped all our gifts for our family, packed our clothes and loaded them in the trunk of Jon's car. We planned on leaving straight from the office on our trip to my folks' home, in order to beat some of the holiday traffic.

When we arrived, Peter came out the front door to help us unload the car. We grabbed each other in a loving embrace as Jon came around the back of the car to give Peter a loving handshake and bro hug. I can't wait to meet Krista, I softly whispered to Peter as we headed to the porch with our packages. She's a beautiful girl, Peter said with such love and admiration. Krista could be the one for Peter, I thought to myself. Dad had opened the door for us, and I got my usual tight squeeze, hug and kiss greeting from my Dad. No matter how old I get, I will always look forward to that special way my Dad greets me each time I come home.

Peter was right, Krista was a beautiful tall slender blond girl. She had the most perfect skin and carried herself with such pride and dignity. I greeted her with a hug and introduced myself. I have heard so much about you Kathryn, I couldn't wait to meet you, she said. Peter had told me of the great childhood you three Collier kids have enjoyed. I was raised in a similar family. We have always served the Lord and trusted Him in our growing up. I can't believe our families are so much alike, Krista continued. I am so happy to have finally met you too Krista, and look forward to many Holidays together, as I gave her a tight hug.

Christmas seemed to fly by, and Jon and I were packing the car to go home. Dad walked out to the car to tell us to be careful and come back real soon. He seemed to have something on his mind as he stood by the back of the car and looked down at the ground. Finally, he took me by the arm and led me a few feet from the car and, again looked down as we stood arm and arm. Then, he began to speak. Kathryn, since you are the oldest and have always looked after your Mother and I these past years, I just want you to take care of your Mother should anything happen to me. I gasped and looked at my Dad in horror. What are you saying Dad, don't talk like that? Mother, the boys and I could never make it without you. Well, I just want you to know everything your Mother and I have is paid for and we also have our burial plans in order, he said in a soft voice. You and Jon can take care of all the legal details. I'm sure your Mother would want to remain here in our home by the river, but she would probably need someone to stay with her. Perhaps you could find a single lady or a widow to stay with your Mother, Dad went on to say. I was standing in a daze as my Dad told me this and I became scared of what our future might be. I don't expect to die real soon Kathryn, but I just wanted you to know this before the Lord comes to take me home. Now don't go home and worry yourself to death about what I have told you, but sometimes people don't take care of details until it's too late. I know Dad, but I can't imagine life without you. You can rest assured, should anything happen to you, the boys and I will make sure Mother is cared for. Dad gave me a tight squeeze and kissed me on my head, as Jon and I got into the car and headed back home.

I couldn't get Dad's conversation off my mind, but as more work piled up at the office, I began to push our conversation back and concentrate on our Court Cases. Our Firm had grown so much that Jon and Curtis had added three more Attorneys to the Firm and two more secretaries. We also had added on to our office in the back and put on three more offices, two more restrooms and increased the size of our small kitchen. Our business was going great and Jon and I were enjoying the fruits of our labor. We had finally finished furnishing the house and had set up one of the upstairs bedrooms into a sweet nursery, with hopes we would soon be blessed again.

Chapter 34

Peter & Krista

Spring was upon us and we had planned to go to my parents' home for Easter. Peter and Krista were also planning to be there. I was excited about getting to see them again as we had not been together since Christmas.

I wanted to tell Peter what Dad had told me when we were leaving after the Christmas Holiday. I was not sure if Dad had told Peter and Brady what he had told me, but I wanted them to know.

When we all arrived at my parents' home, unloaded our cars and were in the house, Peter called us all to the living room and said he had something to say. Excited with what I thought he was going to tell us; I couldn't wait to hear his announcement.

As he stood in the middle of the room, we waited for Mother to come from the kitchen as she wiped her hands on her apron. What is it Peter, we can't wait to hear, Mother said? Krista, come stand by me, Peter said as he grabbed her around the waist and pulled her close to him. Well, he said as

THE RIVER OF LIFE

he looked down into Krista's face, we are in love and I have asked this beautiful girl to be my wife. I can't wait until we are married and find ourselves a home. We have already told Krista's parents and they are pleased to have me for their son-in-law.

Halleluiah! I shouted as I jumped to my feet and grabbed them both. Peter and Krista, I am so happy. You make a wonderful couple and I'm sure you will have a great life with lots of kids. Mother, Dad and Jon joined me with congratulations to the newly engaged couple, as we danced around the room hugging each other. Peter and Krista had planned an early Fall wedding and we were all excited for the upcoming event.

Summer rolled around and Jon and I planned to go visit the folks for Mother's Day. Brady would be coming home, as well as Peter and Krista.

We had planned a little surprise Day for Mother. Krista, Mother and I were all having a full day of beauty. I had made the appointments for nails, pedicures, massages, facials and hair-do's. I knew this would be special for my Mother as she had never felt she and Dad could ever afford anything as extravagant as this day of special treatment.

My mother has had a hard life but if you asked her, she would tell you she has had a very good life, and she and my Dad have been very happy and content as they were raising us kids. They both worked hard, but enjoyed their home, their Church and their kids. That is the life I want Jon and I to give to our family. Children don't have to be showered with expensive gifts, just a loving Christian home and a good education are the most important things you can give them. Jon and I are on the same page as far as raising our family in a loving Christian home. That's the way we were both raised, and we are thankful for it.

Finally fall had arrived and so did the day of Peter and Krista's wedding. We were all excited and those two couldn't have looked more beautiful and happier. The wedding went off without a hitch. They left immediately after the wedding for their 'secret destination' honeymoon.

I had not had a chance to tell Peter what Dad had told me after last Christmas. It never seemed to be a good time to talk with him, I surely didn't want to tell him before his wedding and honeymoon. The right time would come and when it does, I would share the news with both my brothers.

Chapter 35

Good News

Our work at the Law Firm kept both Jon and I on a steady pace, so much so that I had become so fatigued I was leaving the office a couple of hours early each day. We had trained one of the girls in the office to take some of my case work so I wouldn't go to Court so often. This gave me a much-needed break. My fatigue seemed to increase and there were days I was just too tired to even go to the office. Jon had urged me to see the Dr. as perhaps I was low on vitamins or iron and just needed a pick me up. I finally agreed he could be right and called my primary care office to make an appointment. They could see me next Tuesday at 2:00 p.m. That would be good as I always needed to be in the office all day on Monday.

When Tuesday approached, I was more than ready to see my Dr. As usual they ran some tests including blood work, urine, weight, and a complete history of my past few months by asking 'how have you been feeling' questions. After my

THE RIVER OF LIFE

visit with the Dr. and before checking out, the front office nurse told me they would contact me when my tests results were back and schedule me for another appointment. Although, I knew this was the right thing to do to see the Dr., I didn't know any more than when I arrived at his office. I will wait for the test results and go from there. He will probably put me on a lot of vitamins, iron and other medications. I have never been a big fan of taking meds, perhaps that's my downfall.

A week passed and the nurse called me letting me know the tests were back and asked if I could come into the office the next day at 11:00 a.m. I said I could. I told the girls at our front office I would be leaving work at 10:30 a.m. tomorrow. I also told them if anyone had any questions concerning any of my cases, they would need to get with me before my scheduled appointment. They all seemed concerned with my noticeable fatigue and were glad to do anything to take part of my work load.

When my appointment time came, I grabbed my hand bag, told the girls I would see them tomorrow, kissed Jon on my way out the back of his office and got into my car.

My mind was racing as I wondered what could be making me so exhausted. I had never let my mind think 'could this be something serious', but now I was thinking about how Mrs. Barrett was so tired and fatigued before she found out she had Lymphoma. I pulled into a parking space behind the Dr.'s office and sat there for a moment. All at once I was wondering what if this was cancer. I

Good News

then remembered what we always did when we had health issues or difficulties, we would immediately pray and ask God for healing and comfort and to be able to accept whatever came our way. As I held on tight to the steering wheel, I began to ask God to be with me and to help me understand the outcome of my visit with the Doctor.

I got out of my car, went into the building, walked to the front desk, registered and sat down in the waiting room. It was only a few minutes before they called my name and I followed an attractive young nurse into a small examination room. She asked me to sit on the end of the table as she took my blood pressure, and temperature. She laid my file on the desk and told me the Dr. would be in shortly. I thanked her and gazed around the room at the Dr. certificates neatly framed and hung around the walls.

After what seemed like a long wait, Dr. Blackman finally opened the door, extended his hand to greet me and asked how I was feeling. Well I began, not any better. I am just so tired every day, I struggle to work. I am always looking for a place to sit down and can't wait until I get home in the afternoon to lie down on the couch. I was wondering if my tests showed anything significant that could pin-point my fatigue.

After he opened my file and slowly begin to study my test results, the Doctor said, Well, I can tell you one thing Mrs. Davis and that is this, you will feel much better in a few months. In fact, I'm surprised you didn't suspect my findings. What do you mean Dr.? I said with a questioning remark.

THE RIVER OF LIFE

Well, Mrs. Davis, you are expecting a baby. Are you sure Dr.? I quickly questioned. Yes, I am very sure. Your blood and urine test both came back positive for pregnancy, as he continued to scan my file. And you never suspected you were expecting a baby? No, not at all Dr. Blackman, Remember. I was pregnant about 1½ years ago and was so nauseous, I couldn't function. I was a little tired, but the morning sickness was my worse symptom. Unfortunately, as you know, I lost my baby at about 10 weeks.

This time, I was not nauseous just totally fatigued so much so it has consumed my life. Why am I not experiencing morning sickness this time? Well, Dr. Blackman said as he laid my file on the desk in front of him, crossed his arms and began answering my question. All pregnancies are different. A woman can have ten children and maybe not one of the pregnancies will affect her the same way. I want to refer you to one of our best OBGYN Drs. He is in this building on the third floor. His name is Dr. MacPherson. I will have my nurse walk your file up to him and have the front office set up an initial appointment for you. They will contact you for your first visit with Dr. Mac., as we all call him. Thank you very much Dr. Blackman I said, as we shook hands before I left and walked to my car. I was both in a state of shock and overcome with excitement as I got into the car, grasped the steering wheel and began to Praise God and thank him for the wonderful news I had just received. I took this time to also ask for a successful pregnancy, an easy delivery and especially a healthy

Good News

baby. Jon and I would not be too picky about what we would have, boy or girl, just as long if it's healthy. I arrived back home and called Jon. I didn't want to tell him my news over the phone but did tell him the Dr. was pleased with my tests results and would be prescribing some medication. I just failed to say they would be prenatal medications.

I was fixing our dinner when I heard Jon pull into the garage.

He walked in, sit his brief case down, and took off his jacket. He came to the stove and gave me a tight hug. Well honey, he asked, what all did the Dr. have to say about your fatigue?

Well, Jon, you might want to sit down for this news, as I stopped stirring the pan I had on the stove and walked over and sat down at the kitchen table with him. It looks like we are being blessed with a baby. What? Are you serious Kathryn?

How did we miss the signs? I am so excited and happy, this is the best news, as he jumped from his chair and literally picked me up and swung me around the kitchen. Oh Kathryn, I can't wait to tell everyone the news, but I suppose we should wait for a few weeks before we tell anyone, right? Jon said, as he was still jumping around the room. Yes, I think that is a good idea. However, I do feel so different this time, perhaps that's a good sign.

Later that night when we went to our room to go to bed, Jon and I both knelt to thank God for this blessing and to again ask Him for a healthy baby.

I had gotten a call from Dr. Mac's office advising me they had scheduled my first OB appointment for the next week. I was glad to be able to see the

THE RIVER OF LIFE

Dr. in hopes he could give me something for my fatigue, I just needed to feel better in order to continue to work at the Firm.

Finally, my appointment time came, and I was very pleased with my first visit. I had gotten a good report about everything and would see the Dr. again in six weeks, unless something unusual happened. When the first 12 weeks had passed, we told everyone at the firm. They were all happy and excited for us. It was good to know we were over the crucial first trimester when losing the baby was a possibility. The next weekend we went to both of our parents' homes and shared the news with my and Jon families. Everyone was so excited for us and could not wait for our precious one to arrive.

Chapter 36

Baby Arrived

The next few months went quickly, and I felt wonderful. Jon and I had added a few more items to the nursery, had purchased some baby clothes etc., had our bag packed and were in a waiting mode. I had quit going into the office the previous six weeks before my due date and just stayed home to rest. Finally, on June 6, we welcomed our daughter into the world. She weighed 7 lbs. 10 oz. and was very healthy, we named her Camilla Ann Davis. What a blessing she was, and we thanked God every day for giving us this wonderful little girl to raise.

I stayed home with Camilla for the first year and enjoyed every minute of it. Then, an opportunity arose for us to get this wonderful woman, Della Stanfield to keep Camilla. She was a widow and kept several children in her home. All the kiddo's called her Mam-maw Della. She cooked nourishing food every day, read to them and then in the afternoon, had playtime after they had their naps. Camilla thrived while staying with Mrs. Stanfield.

THE RIVER OF LIFE

When Camilla was 2 1/2, we welcomed another daughter into the world and named her Madeline Astrida Davis. Life could not have been better. Our life was perfect, for which Jon and I thanked the Lord daily.

Chapter 37

Dad Passed Away

When the girls were 8 and 10, my Mother called to tell us my Dad was in the hospital and things didn't look good. We took the girls to Mrs. Stanfield's and rushed to my Dad's side. He lasted three days before he took his last breath and went home to be with the Lord. He had such a peaceful look on his face.

Although my heart was broken, I knew he was happy and at peace. Mother seemed to be doing ok, as she had been preparing herself for this day. I stayed on with her for the next four weeks while Jon went home to take care of the girls. He would take them to school, pick them up after school, feed them, get homework, help with baths, drop them off the next morning for school and the cycle continued during my absence. I would call them every night to get a rundown on how their day went. I missed them terribly, but knew my Mother needed me too. I helped take care of donating Dad's clothes, selling some of his tools and making sure the headstone was in place at the cemetery.

THE RIVER OF LIFE

All this was so final and so hard for both of us, but I knew Dad would have wanted me to help Mother with these details before I went back home. I found a wonderful woman in town who had lost her husband and was willing to move in with Mother and help her. Her name was Mrs. Layton, she was a bit younger than Mother and was very able to help with the garden and housework. I kept my promise to Dad and would check on Mother often and would be driving to see her at least twice a month.

The girl's schedules were so full these days and they continued to advance in school. They were both doing very well, making good grades and were in many activities.

Both girls graduated from college with honors. Camilla became an Attorney like her Dad and Madeline 'Maddie' became a Surgeon. Maddie moved to Portland, Oregon where she landed a fabulous job at the Portland Memorial hospital. Camilla came to work for us at the Firm and did an outstanding job. Both girls married wonderful men and Jon and I couldn't have been more pleased. Camilla and her husband Richard had three children, two sons and one daughter. Maddie and her husband Ben had two daughters.

Chapter 38

Deaths

My mother passed away in her sleep at the age of 92. She had a great life and although I miss her terribly, I know Dad was standing there to greet her when she arrived in heaven. I was 69 when she left us.

Our lives continued and Jon and I remained at the Firm working every day. Business was good, we had moved several years earlier into a larger building and added many more employees to the Firm.

Jon was 70 when he finally decided to retire and take life easy. I was glad, we were both still in good health and ready to enjoy the remainder of our life together. We both loved to garden, and we were constantly digging and planting. We wanted to do a lot of traveling too. We enjoyed cruises and road trips. Life was good with Jon; he was a great husband.

One of our first short trips was to my folk's home and visit the river. It was fall and as usual God didn't disappoint us with the array of beautiful

THE RIVER OF LIFE

colors on the trees lining the bank of our river, it was amazing. The large maple tree close to the river was the most beautiful I had ever seen, the yellows, oranges, and reds were outstanding. We'd had some early fall rains and the river was up, splashing against the bank as if it was trying to come greet us. There is nothing on earth as calming as water flowing down stream amongst a bank full of beautiful trees and with hundreds of birds flitting back and forth.

Jon and I enjoyed several more years of vacation trips and cruises. After returning home from the latest of our trips, we were sitting on the porch relaxing. I had made us some tea and we were reminiscing about our recent trip. Suddenly, the way the sun hit Jon's face made him look a strange color of grey. I had never noticed how pale and drawn he looked as he did at that moment. In the next few months, Jon's health seemed to become more fragile and his looks paler. I finally convinced him to call the Dr. and make an appointment. He agreed. After his visit and many tests, the news we received was not good. Jon had Pancreatic Cancer. How could this be? I asked myself. I was in a state of shock and disbelief. How could I survive without my beloved Jon? Jon fought the cancer hard, but after 10 grueling months, the cancer won, and he went home to be with the Lord.

Jon's funeral was the hardest day of my life, as I had to say goodbye to my true love. The girls and their families were all by my side, and that helped me get through the day, but I didn't know what the rest of my life without Jon would be like.

Deaths

The service was a true testament to Jon's life. These are the Pastor's words: Everyone loved Jon, he was an honest, God fearing man. Jon always put God and his family above all else and will always be remember as a great man of God.

So many friends and extended family members came to say goodbye to Jon and to give their condolences to the girls and me.

As I sat on the front row of the church at Jon funeral, staring at his casket, I could almost hear Jon tell me, "You will be ok Kathryn." I would return to our home Jon and I had shared, not alone, but with the Lord by my side.

God had been so good to Jon, our girls and me. I knew I would be ok and was forever grateful and would not be alone. My memories of my beloved Jon will remain in my heart for the rest of my life.

A few years after Jon went home to be with the Lord, Camilla wrote:

Our Mother, Kathryn Collier Davis passed away at the age of 90. We will miss her terribly, but she couldn't wait to take her place in heaven once more beside our Dad, her beloved husband Jon.

THE END

THE RIVER OF LIFE,
by Mary (Tanner) Cannon

The reason I wrote this book:

My Mother, Mary Erma (Collier) Tanner, had a little sister named Kathryn Collier. In 1927 when my Mother was four years old and Kathryn was two, Kathryn was tragically killed by a farm implement. Although, I never saw a picture of Kathryn or heard any details of her short life, God put it on my heart to write a story about her and give her the life she never lived. My book is fiction, however, some of the events are my own experiences.

I named the book, "The River," even though I have neither lived near a river nor was familiar with one. After speaking with Kathryn's only living sibling, Ronnie Collier who is now 79 and a Pastor of the Gospel, told me he felt the "River" was the 'River of Life.' I now agree with him as this book was completely inspired by God through the Holy Spirit.

My book starts at the end of her life. Kathryn returns home from her husband's funeral, gets in the car and drives to her parent's home where she grew up. She sits down on a stump where a

THE RIVER OF LIFE

beautiful Maple once stood next to the River and begins to reminisce about her life.

Christopher Columbus & Ethel Collier
Approx. 1920